INTER COURSES

an aphrodisiac cookbook

written and designed by
martha hopkins & randall lockridge
food photography by ben fink

TERRACE PUBLISHING

InterCourses: an aphrodisiac cookbook

copyright © 1997 by Terrace Publishing,
a partnership of Martha Hopkins and Randall Lockridge

Terrace Publishing
1224 East Crestwood
Memphis, TN 38119-5014
254.753.2843

written and designed by
Martha Hopkins and Randall Lockridge

food photography by Ben Fink
hair and makeup by Angela Angel
food styling/consulting by Jeff Lehr
editorial consulting by Carol Boker

distributed to the book trade in
the United States and Canada by
LPC Group
1436 West Randolph Street
Chicago, IL 60607
800.626.4330

distributed to the gift trade in
the United States and Canada by
Sourcebooks
121 North Washington, Suite 2
Naperville, IL 60540
800.727.8866

International Standard Book Number
0-9653275-0-7

Library of Congress Catalog Card Number
96-90604

Printed in Hong Kong through Phoenix Offset

Published in the United States by Terrace Publishing
and simultaneously in England and
Australia by Reed Books

First Edition
7 9 10 8 6

FOR TURNER

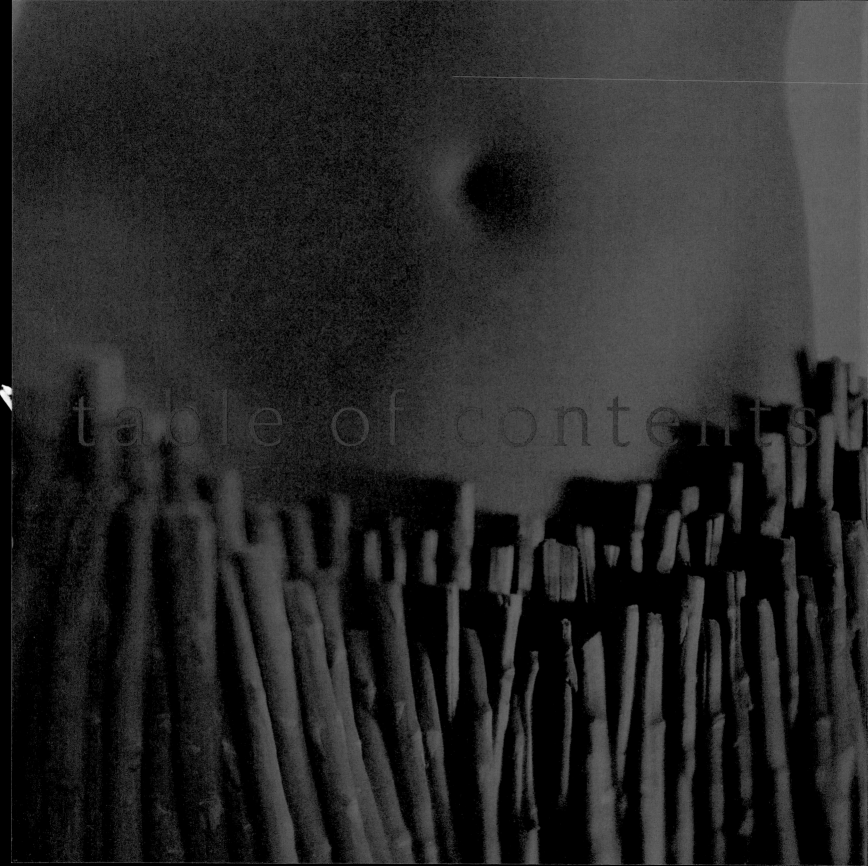

table of contents

introduction to aphrodisiacs . . . 6

massage oils

Recipes for non-edible, but equally sensuous, massage oils and lotions.

aphrodisiacs know no hour

A guide to an InterCourse for any hour of the day.

seducing through the seasons

Selecting the best recipes to capture the gentle chill of fall, the fireplace-warmth of winter, the life of springtime, or the free spirit of summer.

keeping the universe on your side

That classic pick-up line of "Hey baby, what's your sign," takes on new significance in this guide to matching recipes with your partner's astrological sign.

recipes for all stages of the game

Suggests complete menus for every facet in a relationship from the awkward blind date to the comfort and familiarity of a 50-year marriage.

standing alone on the erogenous zones

A map of the human body's most sensitive spots, complete with recipes that work just as well on the body as they do on a plate.

resources

For further exploration.

aphrodisiac

The word itself almost seems magical. On first glance, it conjures up images of Spanish fly, powdered Rhino horn, and other strange, exotic ingredients meant to wield power over unsuspecting souls. • Throughout history, lovers have depended on love potions enhanced with charms of enchantment for those hearts stubborn to cupid's arrow. Sometimes that meant a secret ingredient slipped into a goblet of wine. Other times, an elaborate concoction gulped down for stamina. • The qualifying factors for aphrodisiacs were relatively simple: the rarer an ingredient, the more likely it held aphrodisiacal qualities. Likewise, the more an ingredient resembled a sexual organ, the stronger its power over the libido. • Then inter-continental commerce and science reared their ugly heads. With the emergence of a more global economy, tomatoes quit seeming rare, everybody had access to chocolate, and coffee became a staple of daily life. Science only heightened the situation, stripping age-old aphrodisiacs of their mysterious and powerful qualities. Spanish fly? That simply aggravates the urogenital tract, creating a burning sensation that some associate with the heat of passion. Powdered rhino horn? It comes from a phallic-shaped, nutrient-packed tissue. Other than that, it's power appears only psychological.

bon appétit

chocolate

The Aztecs and Mayans were the first to recognize the potency of chocolate, celebrating the harvest of the cacao bean with festivals of wild orgies. The Aztec ruler, Montezuma, reportedly drank 50 cups of chocolate each day to better serve his harem of 600 women. The belief in chocolate carried on through the Mayan empire where payment for a night at the brothel cost one handful of cacao beans. Seventeenth-century church officials deemed it sinful to partake of chocolate. Casanova, the infamous 18th-century lover, believed in the power of chocolate. And if sales are any indication of our faith in chocolate, then we do too: sales in the 1990s average 600,000 tons of cacao beans consumed each year. • Obviously a tried-and-true staple for lovers, chocolate now has backing from the scientific community. Besides the jolt of caffeine served up in a piece of chocolate, this savory candy also contains PEA, or phenylethylamine, the very same molecule that courses through the veins of one who is in love. Combine our internal stores of this natural amphetamine with chocolate, and one only heightens that giddy sensation known as love.

chocolate-stuffed crescent rolls

easy twist on a french staple

I spent a summer in Paris. It was one of those rare occasions when the experience of something actually outmatches the dream, and memories of the event become a surreal vision in one's mind. While there, I became friends with a man named David. We would often go to a private club he belonged to and dance and laugh and talk all the night long, familiar — as if we had known each other for years. When the club would finally close at 5:00 the next morning, we would stroll to an all-night cafe for strong coffee and a chocolate croissant. This recipe is my quick-and-easy version of the classic French chocolate croissant and a jolt to my memory of our early mornings along the Champs Elysées.

YIELDS 4 ROLLS

2 ounces bittersweet chocolate
1 (4-count) package crescent rolls
1 egg yolk
1 tablespoon milk
2 tablespoons sugar

Cut the chocolate into 4 pieces about 3 inches long. Unfold the crescent roll dough. Place 1 piece of chocolate at the wide end of each piece of dough and roll up. Place on a lightly greased baking sheet. Mix the egg yolk, milk, and sugar in a small bowl. Brush on the rolls, then bake according to package directions. Cool for 15 minutes before eating.

mexican hot chocolate

a classic central american favorite

The best way to experience Mexican hot chocolate is relaxing on a terrace overlooking the heart of Mexico. There, the twinkling lights of the nighttime city will dance for your eyes, and the warmth from the chocolate will embrace you. For a sensual home version, sit in your own backyard under the black sky of night and try a sip from the recipe below.

Y I E L D S   2   S E R V I N G S

Chop the chocolate in a blender or grate by hand. Bring the milk to a boil in a small sauce pan. Pour the hot milk over the chocolate. Using a whisk, hand mixer, or blender, whisk the milk vigorously until the chocolate melts and the milk is frothy. Sprinkle with cinnamon and serve immediately. *Mexican chocolate is available in most Latino markets. If, however, you don't have access to such a specialized place, you can substitute bittersweet chocolate combined with a couple shakes of cinnamon. Feel free to add a touch of sugar to your liking, but know that you won't be drinking authentic Mexican hot chocolate if it's sweet.

3 ounces Mexican chocolate*
3 cups milk or water
  cinnamon for topping

chocolate hazelnut truffles

sweet chocolate dessert candies

Confectioners around the world have long known the exaggerated power of chocolate combined with hazelnuts. And anyone who has ever tasted Baci, the individually wrapped ecstacy of hazelnuts drenched in chocolate or savored a piece of crusty French bread spread thick with creamy Nutella, has an idea of where the following recipe can take you.

Y I E L D S   8   T R U F F L E S

Chop the chocolate in a food processor until finely ground. Add the almond paste and process until smooth. With the motor running, add the coffee and liqueur. Process until the mixture forms a soft ball. Roll mixture into 3/4-inch balls. Sprinkle with the cocoa powder. Place the balls in small paper cups. Chill.

4 ounces bittersweet chocolate
3 1/2 ounces almond paste
1 tablespoon strong hot coffee
1 tablespoon hazelnut liqueur
2 tablespoons cocoa powder

eve's just desserts

red foil

unfolding

to reveal

shapes

beneath

over

longing

to kiss

thin

lying, lips

dark Belgium

conquest

demanding

return

BARRY MCCANN, POMPANO BEACH, FL

black russian cake

a   s e r i o u s   c h o c o l a t e   c a k e

A few years back, my roommate had a crush on one of her classmates. As they worked long, hard hours on a project together, she wooed him to the best of her ability, but he did not seem to be taking the bait. On his end, as is typical of many men, he knew that he liked her, but did she like him? Then she made him this cake. (Well, actually, I made the cake because she had to work the late shift.) Anyway, it's now 4 years later, and they have just purchased their first dog together. It's a pug named Kato, and if he were allowed to eat chocolate, he'd like the cake too.

Y I E L D S   1 2   S E R V I N G S

For the cake, combine the cake mix, oil, pudding mix, eggs, coffee, crème de cacao, and Kahlúa in a large bowl. Beat for 4 minutes until quite smooth. Pour into a greased 10-inch tube pan until three-fourths full. (Save any remaining batter for cupcakes or to simply eat on the spot.) Bake 45 to 50 minutes at 350 degrees. Remove from the pan and invert onto a serving plate. Punch holes throughout the cake with a skewer or ice pick. Prepare the topping by combining the confectioners' sugar, coffee, Kahlúa, and crème de cacao. Mix well and spoon over the warm cake.

Cake:

1 package dark-chocolate cake mix

1 cup vegetable oil

1 (3-ounce) package instant chocolate pudding

4 eggs

3/4 cup strong coffee

1/2 cup crème de cacao

1/4 cup Kahlúa

Topping:

1 cup confectioners' sugar, sifted

2 tablespoons strong coffee

2 tablespoons Kahlúa

2 tablespoons crème de cacao

a s p a r a g u s

These stately stalks first received their aphrodisiac status from the Doctrine of Signatures. Also known as the Law of Similarities, this theory says that if one thing looks like or is reminiscent of another, then it will improve or aid that which it looks like. So if food looks sexual, then the Doctrine of Signatures says it is meant to improve or aid sex. • And indeed, asparagus is a beautiful (albeit slender) phallic symbol. The great French lovers of yesteryear dined on three courses of it on the night before the wedding. According to Diane Ackerman in *A Natural History of Love*, the legendary Hollywood lover of all lovers, Richard Burton, deemed the stalks lascivious. • Today we know that asparagus is packed with potassium, phosphorous, calcium, and vitamin E and offers the love-hungry extra energy, a well-working urinary tract and kidneys, and a natural dose of the "sex vitamin" necessary for increased hormone production.

chicken and asparagus black-bean enchiladas

what tex-mex could be

As this recipe calls for blanched asparagus, you might want to seize this opportunity to make your own version of the asparagus skirt shown at the beginning of the chapter. We promise it's fun. Just trim your asparagus and blanch as usual. Using a needle and substantial thread or lightweight fishing line, thread the asparagus onto the string. Tie around hips and continue preparation of the meal. When it's time for the asparagus to go home to their tortillas, simply pull off with a firm tug, wrap in a tortilla, and bake according to the directions.

YIELDS 2 TO 3 SERVINGS

4   slices bacon

1/2 pound boneless, skinless chicken breasts, cut into thin strips

2   cloves garlic, crushed

1 1/2 cups salsa, divided (note: Paul Newman's salsa is available most everywhere and tastes great — and every penny of profit goes to charity.)

1   (15-ounce) can black beans, undrained

1   small green bell pepper, chopped

1/2 teaspoon ground cumin

1/4 teaspoon chile powder

1/4 cup sliced green onions salt and pepper to taste

6   flour or fresh corn tortillas

3/4 pound blanched asparagus (about 3 stalks per enchilada)

3/4 cup shredded Monterey Jack cheese

1/2 cup light cream

Cook the bacon in a skillet until crisp. Remove from skillet, drain, and crumble. Pour off all but 1 tablespoon bacon drippings. Cook the chicken and garlic in the drippings until tender. Stir in 1/4 cup salsa, beans, bell pepper, cumin, and chile powder. Season with salt and pepper. Simmer for 7 or 8 minutes or until thickened, stirring occasionally. Stir in the green onions and reserved bacon. Spoon the bean mixture down the center of each tortilla. Add 2 to 3 asparagus stalks and top with cheese, reserving 1/4 cup for garnish. Roll up and place, seam side down, in a greased 9x9-inch baking dish. (Can be prepared ahead up to this point and refrigerated until ready to bake.) Combine remaining salsa with cream and pour over the top. Bake at 350 degrees for 15 minutes. Top with remaining cheese. Bake for 5 minutes longer or until cheese melts. Serve with chopped tomatoes, sour cream, and additional salsa.

"The meal seemed to energize my lower chakras, stirring their depths to rise up with impelling, creative force . . ."

Jeff in response to his asparagus frittata and lower-chakras-stirring partner, Isabelle, married 9 years, Memphis, TN

asparagus frittata

make this for brunch-in-bed

Jeff and Isabelle suggest that "before consuming these with gustatory passion, take a moment to contemplate the glistening, firm spears as they rest briefly in their temporary home, waiting to release their life-giving sustenance."

YIELDS 2 SERVINGS

3 eggs, beaten

2 tablespoons chopped
basil leaves

1 clove garlic, finely chopped

2 tablespoons grated
Parmesan cheese, plus
additional for garnish
salt and pepper to taste

¼ pound thin asparagus

2 tablespoons olive oil
basil leaves for garnish

Combine the eggs, basil, garlic, and Parmesan cheese in a bowl. Season with salt and pepper — about ⅛ teaspoon salt, ¼ teaspoon pepper. Let stand for 30 minutes. • Trim the asparagus as described in *pasta with chicken, asparagus, and gorgonzola* (page 19). Steam in a steamer basket or small amount of boiling water until tender, but still bright green. Drain, then season with a few drops of olive oil. Keep warm. • Heat the remaining olive oil in a large skillet over medium-high heat. Pour a ladleful of egg mixture into the pan. Swirl it around the pan. Lower the heat to medium. When frittata turns opaque, flip it over and cook the other side until lightly browned. Repeat with other frittata. Divide the asparagus into 2 bunches. Roll each bunch in a frittata. Garnish with basil and grated cheese.

pasta with asparagus, chicken, and gorgonzola

bold combination of flavors

As is the case with artichokes, many people do not quite know how to approach asparagus. Try this: Trim the asparagus by gently bending each stalk near the base to break off the tough, woody ends. Peel the skin off the bottom 2 inches of any thicker or older stalks using a peeler or paring knife. Your asparagus is now ready for cooking.

YIELDS 2 TO 3 SERVINGS

Trim and clean the asparagus. Cut into 1½-inch lengths. Blanch in boiling water; set aside. Cook the linguine until al dente; drain and set aside. Melt the butter in a large skillet. Stir-fry the chicken until browned. Whisk in the cream, red pepper, shallots, and nutmeg. Add the Gorgonzola cheese; stir until melted. Add the tarragon, asparagus, and linguine. Toss well. Place on a warmed platter. Serve with the Parmesan cheese.

½ pound fresh asparagus
½ pound linguine
1 tablespoon butter
1 cup thin strips chicken (about 1 small breast)
½ cup heavy cream
  red pepper flakes to taste
1½ tablespoons finely chopped shallots
  dash of nutmeg
2 ounces Gorgonzola cheese, crumbled
1 tablespoon fresh tarragon
¼ cup Parmesan cheese

asparagus-prosciutto rolls

easy and delicious

These rolls are good finger food. Sure, the vinaigrette might dribble on your chin and the asparagus might slip out to find itself a new home and the cream cheese might put a white dab on your rosy cheek. As I was saying, these rolls are good finger food.

YIELDS 2 TO 3 SERVINGS

Combine the olive oil, vinegar, mustard, and garlic in a bowl; whisk well. Stir in the chives and salt and pepper. Spread each piece of prosciutto with ½ tablespoon of cheese. Roll 3 stalks of asparagus in each half of prosciutto. Top with vinaigrette. Serve at room temperature.

¼ cup olive oil
1 tablespoon red wine vinegar
½ tablespoon Dijon mustard
1 clove of garlic, crushed
1 tablespoon minced fresh chives
  salt and pepper to taste
3 thin slices prosciutto, cut in half crosswise
3 tablespoons cream cheese or goat cheese, divided
18 stalks asparagus, blanched
  Italian parsley for garnish

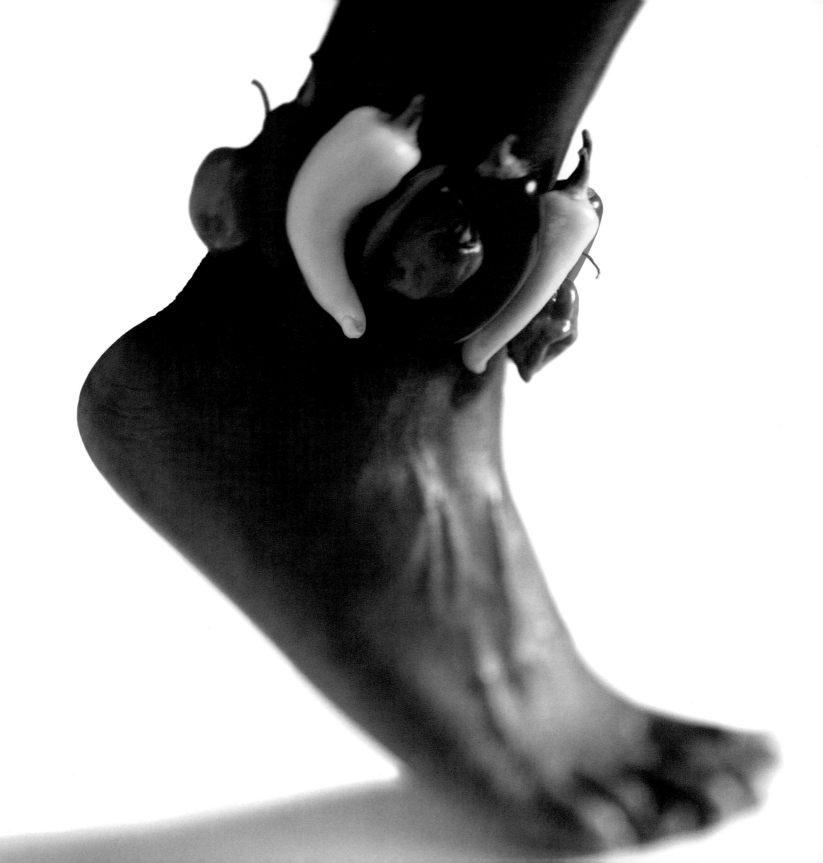

chiles

Long believed to house a complete arsenal of aphrodisiac powers, the chile pepper makes a strong statement to all who taste of its flesh. With more than 200 varieties world wide, chiles seem to have as many options for heating things up as clever lovers do. There's the firecracker hot of the tiny red-orange pequín that explodes in the mouth with the first bite. The heated sweet of the wrinkled pepperoncini. The delayed fireball of the dark-brown chilaca that lurks behind other flavors until it's ready to take charge. The gently pleasing spice of the slender, green Anaheim. • Dr. John Harvey Kellogg, inventor of Corn Flakes and founder of Kellogg cereal company, knew what he was talking about when he advised nymphomaniacs to stay away from peppers. Eating peppers gets the blood rushing, the heart pumping, the face flushing, and the pores sweating — all reactions strangely familiar to what one can experience with anything from a good-night kiss at the front door to a heated quickie during lunch hour.

spicy grilled shrimp

finger-licking good

juice and zest of 2 limes

3 hot chile peppers, seeded and sliced

2 stalks lemon grass, outer leaves removed, sliced

1 (2-inch) piece ginger, grated (about 2 tablespoons)

2 cloves of garlic, crushed

2 tablespoon warm honey

6 tablespoons olive oil

1 tablespoon chopped cilantro

1 pound jumbo shrimp, shelled and deveined

"I'll remember feeding him the spicy flavored shrimp — his tongue trailing my saucy fingers so slowly that I'm positive time stopped. I'll remember him rubbing the spices along my mouth, only to lick them off seconds later. I'll remember lips on fingers, tongues on mouths, heat and honey. And I will never think of grilled shrimp the same way again." *Anne on her experience with spicy grilled shrimp and Eric, 6 dates in 2 weeks, Jacksonville, FL*

Y I E L D S   2   T O   3   S E R V I N G S

Combine the lime juice, zest, chiles, lemon grass, ginger, garlic, honey, olive oil, and cilantro in a bowl; mix well. Add the shrimp, coating well. Refrigerate for 4 hours. Thread on skewers. Grill over medium-high heat for about 5 minutes on each side; brush with marinade while cooking.

come-to-jamaica wings

rum adds a fun dimension to the bite

"First, she said, hot then sweet. Pepper. Honey. Then, she whispered, sweet and then hot. Her hands slid then clutched. They honeyed then peppered. I kept thinking what a wicked, wicked angel."

Walter on how much he loves his spicy wings and his spicier Jane, together 5 months, Boston, MA

Y I E L D S   2   T O   3   S E R V I N G S

¼ cup lime juice

2 tablespoons dark rum

2 tablespoons honey

1 jalapeño pepper, thinly sliced

1 tablespoon soy sauce

3 pounds large chicken wings

Combine lime juice, rum, honey, peppers, and soy sauce. Cut off chicken wing tips and discard. Separate wings at the joint to make 2 sections per wing. Place in a large dish. Pour lime mixture over wings. Add enough water to cover. Refrigerate for 24 hours. Drain wings and pat dry. Grill for 5 to 6 minutes or until done.

thai chicken with peanut sauce

fiery taste, entertaining to roll

Many of my Memphis cohorts epitomize the meat-and-potatoes mentality that infiltrates the South, so I usually have to enjoy Thai food alone. One afternoon, I could not live another minute without a steamy bowl of pho, so I headed to my favorite establishment. Sitting alone, I entertained myself by watching the table across from me: two Thai teenagers, both about 16. They sat across from each other, both leaning back, smoking, and trying to look cool in that way that only 16-year-olds can. Underneath the table, I could see some subtle foot action beginning to unfold — nothing obvious, but enough for a keen voyeur like me to detect. When the food arrived, he picked up a roll, dipped it in the peanut sauce, and fed her. She bit it and smiled. They ditched the cool act and fed each other the entire meal, midst giggles and "inadvertent" touches. And I could see from the look in their eyes that they were in love.

YIELDS 2 TO 3 SERVINGS

To prepare the marinade, combine the soy sauce, garlic, sugar, peanut oil, lime, and ground pepper in a bowl. Rinse the chicken and pat dry. Add to the marinade. Chill, covered, for 1 hour or longer. To prepare the sauce, sauté the garlic and chili paste in the oil for 30 seconds or until the garlic is lightly browned. Add the broth, coconut milk, peanut butter, soy sauce, and sugar; whisk to blend. Bring to a boil, reduce heat, and simmer for 2 minutes to thicken, stirring frequently; cover and set aside. When ready to serve, place in small individual bowls and garnish with the chopped peanuts. Drain the marinade from the chicken. Grill the chicken over a hot fire for 10 minutes or until done. Let stand for 5 minutes, then cut into strips. • To serve, place lettuce, mint, and cilantro leaves on a large platter. Place 1 large lettuce leaf or 1 spring roll wrapper flat. Top with chicken strips, sesame seeds, mint leaves, and cilantro leaves. Roll up lettuce or wrapper, dip in the peanut sauce, and enjoy with some plum wine or Sapparo beer.

Marinade:
1 tablespoon light soy sauce
1/2 teaspoon minced garlic
2 teaspoons sugar
1 tablespoon peanut oil
1 tablespoon lime juice
  grated zest of 1/2 lime
  black pepper to taste
2 boneless, skinless chicken breast halves

Peanut Sauce:
1 teaspoon minced garlic
  pinch of Szechuan hot chili bean paste
2 teaspoons vegetable oil
1/4 cup chicken broth
2 tablespoons unsweetened coconut milk
1 1/2 tablespoons creamy peanut butter
1 teaspoon light soy sauce
  pinch of sugar
1 1/2 tablespoons dry-roasted peanuts, chopped

Serving Ingredients:
  green or red leaf lettuce leaves
  spring roll wrappers
2 tablespoons sesame seeds, toasted
1/2 cup fresh mint leaves
1/2 cup fresh cilantro

salsa oaxaqueño

authentic taste of southern mexico

Oaxaca captured my heart the minute my train chugged into the station. I went there for a summer and lived with a family in a colonia called Indeco Xoxo. My friends and I would often go into town for an evening of salsa — dancing, that is. We would don our new floral skirts, gossamer blouses embroidered in electric colors, and hirachis all bought earlier that week at the big market. And off we would go for an evening of *bailar*, breaking all sorts of mores in this old-school Mexican town. But we were young and hot and hungry, and salsa dancing offered us a taste of relief. The spicy flavors of this recipe capture a bit of how we felt on those Oaxacan nights, dancing on the cobblestones outside our favorite salsa clubs.

2 tomatoes, finely diced
½ red onion, finely diced
½ cup tomato juice
1 tablespoon minced
   chipotle pepper
1 clove garlic, crushed
¼ cup chopped cilantro
   juice of 2 limes
   salt and pepper to taste

YIELDS ABOUT 2 CUPS

Combine the tomatoes, onion, tomato juice, chipotle pepper, garlic, cilantro, and lime juice in a bowl. Season with salt and pepper. Chill, covered, for up to 6 days. Serve with fresh corn tortillas.

"This was the first meal I ever made for my new boyfriend, so I was very excited to see how the meal (and the evening) would go. The shrimp was a very aromatic dish — the lemon grass, garlic, ginger — they all heightened my senses throughout the preparation. We ate the meal by candlelight, enjoying both the food and the company. After dinner, we ran down to the store for some more wine, only to find his apartment robbed when we returned! All aphrodisiac power permanently drained from us (or so I thought), we had to deal with cops, locksmiths, and insurance claims until 2:00 a.m. But when we finally fell into bed, all the stress of the evening behind us, our thoughts once again turned to the shrimp and its hot spicy fiery sizzling heat. And I felt hotter for him than I'd ever felt for anyone before."

Kim on preparing spicy grilled shrimp for Taylor, first at-home dinner, Fairfax, VA

indian-spiced chicken gyro

an intensely flavored experience

1 teaspoon lemon juice

1 teaspoon Balsamic vinegar

½ cup plain yogurt

1 teaspoon chopped
fresh ginger

½ teaspoon crushed garlic

½ teaspoon chopped cilantro

¼ teaspoon ground cumin

¼ teaspoon cayenne pepper

¼ teaspoon turmeric

3 boneless, skinless chicken
breast halves

2 whole pita rounds

3 leaves red or green
leaf lettuce

½ cup peeled, thinly
sliced cucumber

mint mayonnaise

I met a boy in Paris who played table tennis. Competed, even, and won. I first met him and his sandy hair and dreamy eyes in front of Notre Dame. But it is my last night out with him, some weeks later, that relates to the gyro and my own personal happiness. • We were wandering about the streets of Paris, trying to decide where to go, but not really deciding much of anything. We happened by a gyro stand; he bought a gyro for himself and stole an orange for me from the fruit stand next door. We wandered a bit farther until we came upon an old church with wide front steps. There we sat, he with his gyro on one step, me with my orange on the step below. Between bites, he murmured something that I couldn't quite catch. I turned my head to look back over my shoulder and ask him what he'd said. But instead of repeating his comment, he caught my head in the crook of his elbow and kissed me, sweet and light, the citrus taste of my lips mixing with the spicy coating on his. I felt that unassuming kiss down to my toes.

YIELDS 2 TO 3 SERVINGS

Combine the lemon juice, vinegar, yogurt, ginger, garlic, cilantro, cumin, cayenne, and turmeric in a bowl; mix well. Pour over the chicken in a shallow dish. Cover and refrigerate for up to 8 hours. Grill the chicken over medium-high heat or sauté on the stove until done. Heat the pita rounds to make a sandwich using the chicken, lettuce, cucumber, and *mint mayonnaise*.

mint mayonnaise

great on the daily turkey sandwich, too

½ cup loosely packed
fresh mint leaves

½ cup loosely packed
fresh cilantro

¼ cup alfalfa sprouts

½ jalapeño pepper, minced

1½ tablespoons chopped onion

1 teaspoon cider vinegar

¼ cup mayonnaise

YIELDS ABOUT 3/4 CUP

Combine the mint leaves, cilantro, sprouts, jalapeño, and onion in a food processor; process until finely chopped. Add the vinegar and mayonnaise just until blended.

honey-peppered salmon

simple to prepare

"I met her on the Internet in the Missouri room. You always read about those people who say they're

blond, 5'10", beautiful women, but they're really hairy-backed, 5'4" men with strange habits. But

after e-mailing each other for several weeks, then telephoning for several more weeks, we decided to

risk that each other might be a crazed freak and actually meet. We broke all the rules of meeting a

stranger — didn't tell anyone else we were meeting, met at a quiet restaurant — pretty stupid, I guess,

but it all seemed so exciting and mysterious that neither of us cared. Oh man, she was everything I

had imagined, only more beautiful, more intelligent, more thoughtful, more sensual, more more more.

At first, we couldn't even talk, only stare into each other's eyes in disbelief that this was really

happening. And although we barely touched our dinner of salmon, testing this recipe brought back

all the feelings I had that night when we talked and shared and gazed and smiled until we couldn't

stand it any longer. We didn't sleep together that night. Somehow it would've spoiled it. But we held

each other tight until the sun came up and I had to drive my 3 hours back home for work. We had

an excruciatingly intense relationship for about the next six weeks. It didn't work out — right chemistry,

wrong timing. I still think often of her." *Jeremy, Kansas City, MO*

YIELDS 2 SERVINGS

Combine the olive oil, honey, mustard, garlic, cayenne, coriander, lemon juice, and salt in a shallow dish. Mix well. Add salmon steaks and let marinate for 30 minutes at room temperature. Place the salmon in a greased baking dish. Bake at 350 degrees for 6 to 7 minutes per side. Garnish with dill sprigs

1/4 cup olive oil
1 tablespoon honey
2 tablespoons Dijon mustard
3 cloves garlic, peeled and minced
2 teaspoons cayenne
1/2 teaspoon ground coriander
2 tablespoons lemon juice
salt to taste
2 (6-ounce) salmon steaks
dill sprigs for garnish

c o f f e e

Nothing beats a cup of joe. It's everywhere, all the time. It probably became an aphrodisiac by default. We drink it in the morning to wake up. We drink it after dinner to close the meal. We have coffee in bed, on the couch, at the table. We mix it with cream or sugar or cream and sugar or honey, no cream please. We ice it down when we're hot. We froth it up when we're vogue. We drink regular, decaffeinated, imported, gourmet, flavored, blended. We use instant granules for speed, percolators for the richest taste, and a programmable drip for a Monday morning alarm. Whether in fine china or a mug, a demitasse or tall Italian glass, coffee is an aphrodisiac we use daily. • Who knows why anyone first believed the coffee bean enhanced love? Maybe it's the dark, rich color of a freshly brewed pot. Or its pleasingly bitter scent wafting through the air. Or the jolt of caffeine it pumps through our blood. Or maybe it's just because when you offer someone coffee, you are welcoming them to sit down and stay awhile. And friendliness is *always* attractive.

"the buttery-brown liquid

our porch.

reminded me of his perfect

our swing.

skin as I sat sandy-eyed

his bathrobe, my cup.

and blissful on our porch."

rondalyn on drinking coffee and her michael, together 7 months, atlanta, ga

frozen coffee almond dessert

enticingly cold and smooth

"Testing this recipe with Patrick brought back a flood of memories of the days we first met. I was out one hot July night walking home with a friend, and we passed an outdoor coffee shop called the Pop Stop. I saw a guy sitting at a table alone, his feet up on a drain. Our eyes met, and as I passed, I waited a few seconds, turned — he did the same — and we gave each other a huge smile. • I placed an ad in the 'glances' section the next week (my first classified I might add): *'Pop Stop 7/6. You — sitting outside at a table alone. Me — walking by with a friend. We exchanged smiles, how about phone numbers?'* Two days later, he called. He was so excited, sincere, even a little innocent — something you don't find these days. We met for ice cream, talked for hours, and had our first kiss. It was wonderful. • As I wrote him a bit later, 'Here's to coffee shops, ice cream, and classifieds.'"

Patrick and Tracy, in love for 2 months, Washington, DC

YIELDS 4 TO 6 SERVINGS

Crumble the macaroons together with the graham crackers. Mix with the rum and Kahlúa in a small bowl. Line the bottom of a small freezer-proof serving dish with the mixture.

Layer the ice cream, then the chocolate, then the whipped cream over the macaroons. Sprinkle with the almonds. Freeze at least 2 hours to set.

6 almond-macaroon cookies
6 chocolate graham crackers
3 tablespoons rum
3 tablespoons Kahlúa
1 quart coffee ice cream, softened
1/2 cup shaved dark chocolate
6 ounces whipping cream, whipped
1/2 (4-ounce) package sliced almonds, toasted

espresso cream

ricotta flavored with coffee and brandy

"It was a highly unusual dish with spectacular after effects. There's enough Baylor University left in me to be reticent about the particulars, but let's just say that the earth shook and the heavens cried out. Sorry, but that's all the detail you get." *Ben and Julia, together 6 years, St. Paul, MN*

YIELDS 2 SERVINGS

1½ cups ricotta cheese, drained

¼ cup cream

2 tablespoons freshly ground espresso coffee beans

2 to 3 tablespoons sugar

4 teaspoons brandy

2 tablespoons chopped, toasted almonds

2 tablespoons chocolate-covered espresso beans

Combine the ricotta and cream, beating until smooth. Stir in the coffee beans, sugar, and brandy. Cover and chill for at least 3 hours.

Before serving, garnish with toasted almonds and chocolate-covered espresso beans.

hot mocha chocolate

a dessert in itself

As Aaron tells it, "I was in New York for the weekend and went by one of my favorite galleries to see what they were showing. While there, a girl named Dominique walked over to me and introduced herself. Considering how shy I am with strangers, it's a good thing she made the first move. We started talking, went to an auction, continued talking, went window shopping, kept on talking, and decided to go down the street for some coffee. We sank down into one of the cafe's big, fluffy sofas and, over a cup of hot mocha chocolate, I found out she was a millionaire many times over. I've always considered that I got lucky that night — just on a different level than usual."

YIELDS 2 SERVINGS

Combine the cornstarch and ½ cup of the milk, stirring until smooth. Place in a double-boiler with the remaining milk, cream, coffee, and sugar. Cook over medium-high heat until thickened, stirring frequently. Simmer, covered, for 10 minutes. Add ½ cup hot coffee mixture to the egg in a bowl, beat constantly. Pour the egg mixture into the remaining coffee mixture in a pan, mixing well. Simmer, covered, for 2 minutes. Pour into coffee mugs, garnish, and serve.

2 tablespoons cornstarch

1½ cups milk

½ cup heavy cream

1¼ tablespoons instant
 coffee granules

¼ cup sugar or to taste

1 egg, beaten
 whipped cream, chocolate-
 covered espresso beans,
 and shortbread cookies
 for garnish

b a s i l

Considered the royal herb of the Greeks and a sacred herb in India, the alluring power of basil has been used for centuries to keep wandering eyes focused homeward. Early on, says Vera Lee in *Secrets of Venus*, wives with straying husbands "powdered their breasts with pulverized basil." Haitian lore claims basil comes from Erzulie, their goddess of love. And today, some therapists use the essential oil of basil to treat the Madonna/whore complex. • But it's more than its history or essential oil that makes basil an aphrodisiac. It's the beauty of a healthy basil plant, with its buttery leaves painting a background of green for its white flowers. Once picked, its fragrant scent seasons a plain strand of pasta, adds a third dimension to a simple garden salad, and makes a frozen pizza almost edible. • Celebrate basil. Make a laurel of purple and green leaves dotted in basil flowers. Don flowing white clothes. Run through a field of wild flowers and tumble to the ground with your partner, kissing until you can no longer.

grilled scallops with basil and lavender essence

simple ingredients, complex flavor

To introduce your taste buds to a whole new realm of senses, consider incorporating essential oils into your cooking. Essential oil is just that — the very essence of a particular flower, plant, or other botanical. In this case, Spencer Krenke with Aromatherapy of Rome recommends adding lavender essence to the simple classic of sautéed scallops or shrimp for a complex mixture of flavors with each bite.

YIELDS 2 TO 3 SERVINGS

15 to 20 fresh basil leaves
1 clove garlic
1 teaspoon salt
1/4 teaspoon pepper
2 drops essential oil of lavender
2 tablespoons olive oil
6 large sea scallops (about 1 pound)

Combine the basil, garlic, salt, and pepper in a blender or food processor; process until smooth. Add the 2 drops of lavender essential oil to 1 tablespoon of the olive oil, then add to the processed mixture. Let stand for 30 minutes. Cut a deep horizontal slit through the scallops, but not the whole way through. Fill with the basil mixture; close with a wooden pick. Drizzle with the remaining 1 tablespoon olive oil. Grill for 2 to 3 minutes on each side. (Note: please see page 139 of the resources for more information on purchasing essential oils. Never substitute a true essential oil with a less-expensive, synthetic version.) If lavender oil is unavailable, sprinkle the grilled scallops with fresh lemon juice.

basil-eggplant soup

filling and hearty

After three years in the Peace Corps, Sam and Bev live quite the minimalist lifestyle. They operate in a fully-equipped kitchen, complete with one wooden spoon, one small paring knife, one stock pot, and a cast-iron griddle. Regardless, they found this recipe's taste well worth their cooking detours caused by a life sans grill or blender. They enjoyed their soup from their tiny balcony which, with the help of the nighttime stars, made for a quaint dining experience.

YIELDS 2 TO 3 SERVINGS

Grill the eggplant until charred and tender. Cut in half lengthwise, scoop out the pulp and discard the skin. (Or, if you prefer, peel and dice the eggplant, then boil in a small amount of salted water until tender.) Sauté the onion, garlic, and oregano in 3 tablespoons of the olive oil in a saucepan until the onion is tender. Add the eggplant, tomatoes, chicken stock, salt and pepper, and cayenne. Simmer, partly covered, for 35 minutes. Purée the basil in a blender with the remaining 2 tablespoons oil. Blend in the goat cheese; set aside. Purée the eggplant soup in the blender. Spoon into bowls. Serve with a dollop of basil paste.

1 medium eggplant (about 1 pound)
1 small onion, finely minced
1 large clove garlic, crushed
1/2 tablespoon minced oregano
5 tablespoons olive oil, divided
3 or 4 large ripe Italian plum tomatoes, peeled, seeded, and chopped
1 1/2 cups chicken stock
salt and pepper to taste
pinch of cayenne pepper
1 cup packed fresh basil, washed, dried
2 ounces goat cheese

honey-glazed salmon

a simple treatment for a beautiful fish

Aaron likes, rather loves, salmon. Remember his experience at the cafe in the Village? Well, in follow-up, they decided to rendezvous in New York again. He flew in from Texas, she from Boston. They were to meet at a hip New York restaurant, not having seen each other since that night at the cafe six months before. In Aaron's words, "She ran into the restaurant, 30 minutes late, soaking wet from the rain, with luggage in tow. Once she regrouped and warmed up, I ordered the baked salmon and she ordered a noodle-basket with shrimp called Aphrodisiac Love Nest. Hubba hubba. I'm not telling anymore, but yes, I do still call her."

YIELDS 2 SERVINGS

2   (6-ounce) salmon fillets
    salt and pepper to taste
2   teaspoons honey
2   teaspoons chopped basil

Rinse the salmon and pat dry. Place, skin-side down, in a greased baking dish. Season with salt and pepper. Coat with the honey and top with the basil. Bake at 350 degrees for 15 minutes or until done (about 10 minutes per inch of thickness). May substitute or add other herbs of your choice for the basil.

summertime cucumber sandwiches

light and cool for sultry days

These sandwiches go with lemonade and front porches. First kisses and hot days. Ceiling fans and tree swings. Picnics and wildflowers. They can take you back to the days of innocence and discovery. When mom made cucumber sandwiches for you and the boy down the street, and he touched your hand while she trimmed the final crust from the bread.

YIELDS 6 SMALL SANDWICHES

¼   cup mayonnaise
1   teaspoon cider vinegar
    pinch of salt
1   teaspoon each chopped
    fresh parsley, oregano,
    thyme, basil, dill, chives
1   teaspoon minced onion
    garlic salt, Worcestershire
    sauce, chile powder,
    and cumin to taste
12 slices white bread
1   cucumber, peeled
    and sliced
    fresh dill or parsley
    for garnish

Combine the mayonnaise, vinegar, salt, herbs, onion, and additional seasonings in a small bowl. Mix well. Chill, covered, overnight. Cut bread rounds out of slices. Spread with the herb mixture. Place a slice of cucumber on each round and top with another round.

In preparation for the
tomato-basil soup, Jeff suggests,

"Before chopping the
tomatoes, take time to
appreciate the feeling of
their round shapes and
smooth skins. Close your
eyes and pass them between
yourself and your partner,
slowly, carefully. Let your
imagination go . . ."

tomato-basil soup

a heart-warmer

Jeff enjoyed his tomato-basil soup: "This luscious soup offered us everything we could ever want in a tasteful prelude to an amorous evening encounter: the wonderful smell of onions, garlic, and basil wafting through our home as they simmered; the smooth, rich texture and warm layers of flavor cascading from lips to tongues to throats, then bellies. Finally, the surprisingly sensuous effect of good (try sourdough!) French bread, soaked through with velvety, herb-laden liquid, giving nourishing sustenance to a light, energizing meal. Afterward: untold delights."

YIELD 2 TO 3 SERVINGS

1 small onion, chopped
2 or 3 cloves garlic, chopped
1 tablespoon olive oil
1 pound (about 3 medium)
   tomatoes, chopped
1/2 cup tomato sauce
3/4 cup chicken broth
1/4 cup cream
2 tablespoons coarsely
   chopped basil
1 slice well-toasted country
   bread
2 tablespoons grated
   Parmesan cheese
   salt and pepper to taste
   pesto (optional)

Sauté the onion and garlic in olive oil in a skillet until tender. Add the tomatoes. Cook over medium heat for 10 minutes. Add the tomato sauce, broth, cream, and half of the basil. Simmer for 30 minutes. Process in a blender until smooth. Return to the pan. Add the bread, remaining basil, and Parmesan cheese. Season with salt and pepper. Garnish with additional cheese, oil, and pesto if desired.

basil frittata hero

yellow petals accented with green basil

"If thou dost love fair Hero, cherish it, . . .

And thou shalt have her." Don Pedro, *Much Ado About Nothing*

Y I E L D S   2   S E R V I N G S

Combine the eggs, milk, marjoram, basil, green onion, and cheese in a bowl. Season with salt and pepper. Mix well. Heat the olive oil in a small nonstick skillet. Prepare 6 thin frittatas using the directions on page 18. Cut the rolls in half horizontally and spread with aïoli. ("O Hero, what a Hero hadst thou been.") Stack 3 frittatas in each roll. Top with the shredded garnish and the other half of the roll. ("Sweet Hero! now thy image doth appear in the rare semblance that I loved it first." Claudio, *Much Ado About Nothing*.)

Partake of the beautiful sandwich.

3 eggs, beaten

2 teaspoons milk

1 teaspoon chopped fresh marjoram

1 tablespoon chopped fresh basil

1 green onion, finely chopped

2 tablespoons freshly grated Parmesan or Romano cheese
  salt and pepper to taste

2 teaspoons olive oil

2 French bread rolls

1½ tablespoons aïoli or garlic-flavored mayonnaise, divided
  shredded spinach and basil for garnish

g r a p e s

Considered one of the first fruits, these luscious spheres we know as grapes produce many things fine and good. Try to imagine a world without grapes. Certainly, some substitutions will work. No more home-canned muscadine jelly for your buttermilk biscuits? Try strawberry jam. No more rich juice to sip? Apple will suffice. No more pale-green, ruby-red, or midnight-purple clusters for the artist's still life? Pears are pretty. No more grape vine to swirl about your fresh-cut flowers? How about some wheat stalks or ferns? No more Chardonnay or Beaujolais or Pinot Noir or port or champagne or sherry or vermouth? That's okay, you can distill some elderberries in your backyard. No more plump bites of juice and sweet that squirt a fountain of aphrodisiacal power and grape flavor into your mouth? That's right. No more. Oh, to shudder at the thought of such a sad existence. Savor your grapes. Appreciate them well.

grape sorbet

so cool, so cleansing

For a luscious ruby-red dessert and refreshing end to a fiery meal, cool down with this grape sorbet. According to Jon and Caroline, together 29 years in Birmingham, AL, it "leaves a sweet nectar aftertaste on the tongue that has you begging for more."

3 pounds red or black
   seedless grapes, stemmed
2 tablespoons lemon juice
1/3 cup sugar
1/4 cup wine

Purée the grapes in a food processor. Strain the juice through a sieve, pressing with the back of a spoon to remove all juice. Heat the juice in a saucepan. Add the lemon juice, sugar, and wine, stirring until the sugar dissolves. Check sweetness and adjust if necessary. Chill, covered. Freeze in ice cream machine or in freezer, stirring occasionally to keep crystals from forming.

cabernet sauvignon ice

earthy flavor

"We had just taken Mollie, our 2-year-old black lab for a walk on the banks of the Mississippi near our house. She exudes life, and expects everyone to come along with her — even when it's 90 degrees with 90 percent humidity. When she finally wore out (long after we had worn out), she allowed us to return home to our ceiling fan, slingback chairs, and cabernet sauvignon ice from the night before. The refreshingly non-sweet slush just about sent us over the edge. We ended up sitting in our slingbacks, talking and sipping the snowflakes of ice until the sun went down over the river."

Marilyn and Tom, married 26 years, Memphis, TN

1/2 cup water
1/2 cup sugar
3/4 cup Cabernet Sauvignon
3/4 cup white grape juice
1/3 cup lemon juice
     red grapes and mint
     sprigs for garnish

Combine the water, sugar, and wine in a saucepan. Bring to a boil. Reduce heat and simmer for 5 minutes; cool. Add the grape juice and lemon juice. Cover and chill for 1 hour. Pour into a divided ice cube tray. Freeze until solid (about 4 hours). Place cubes, one at a time, in a food processor. Process until slushy. Serve in sherbet dishes garnished with grapes and mint.

sausages with grape sauce

plump links complemented by sweet grapes

As Susan tells it, "Once David quit making jokes about the sausage links and started tasting them instead, the evening turned round in my favor. I was at the stove and had just finished adding the grapes to the sauce. I dipped my finger in it for a taste test to adjust the seasonings, but he stopped my hand mid route to my mouth. When he took it on a detour to *his* mouth, I knew it was going to be a good evening." *Susan and David, together 3 years, Anaheim, CA*

YIELDS 3 TO 4 SERVINGS

Boil the sausages in water to cover for 12 to 15 minutes or until no longer pink; drain. Sprinkle the bottom of a greased 1-quart baking dish with the shallots. Arrange the sausages on top. Cover with wine. Bake at 425 degrees for 35 to 40 minutes, turning sausages to brown evenly.

Remove sausages but keep warm. Move the baking dish to the stove on medium-low heat. Whisk in the mustard. Add the grapes, stirring until warmed. Season to taste. Pour over the sausages. Top with the parsley and serve with toast points.

4 links sweet Italian sausage
(about 3/4 pound)

1 shallot, minced

3/4 cup dry white wine

1 tablespoon Dijon mustard

1/2 cup seedless grapes, halved
salt and pepper to taste

1 1/2 tablespoons
minced parsley

pasta with grapes

fruit and cheese plate meets pasta

Give your partner a quick jolt of Mae West seduction and peel them grapes!

YIELDS 3 SERVINGS

Toss the cheese, grapes, watercress, scallions, orange juice and zest, salt and pepper,

hot pasta, and olive oil in a large bowl.

Serve immediately.

2 ounces goat cheese,
cut into small wedges

4 ounces seedless
white grapes

1 bunch watercress, trimmed
and coarsely shredded

2 scallions, chopped
juice and zest
of 1/2 orange
salt and pepper to taste

6 ounces pasta spirals,
cooked

2 tablespoons olive oil

Henry and I couldn't believe it. As the recipe instructs, I prepared the pasta last, and served it immediately (with garlic breadsticks, Gamay Beaujolais, and sliced garden tomatoes). The meal was wonderful, very romantic. Lots of talking and long glances over the table full of luminous dishes. We had both eaten quite a bit more than we were known to, and had just leaned back in our chairs to relax, finish the wine, and exchange a languid smile, when a particularly slender piece of pasta stood up, bowed to a sprig of watercress (who, we think, responded with a curtsy) and began to dance the tango. It was rough going until they worked their way down the plate (away from the grapes who were, at this point, very worked up and, with all their shimmying, had made the dance floor quite perilous) and onto the tablecloth. It was on the table that they really let loose, dipping, twirling, and seducing each other until they fell, exhausted, onto the butterplate in a fit of giggles and kisses.

Jen and Henry on their amazing experience of pasta with grapes

grapes rolled in almonds and ginger

cleopatra would be proud

Concerning these voluptuous jewels, Jim wrote, "Laurel said this one was fun — need I say more? If we can get her smiling, the road to ecstasy is not far away." (Especially if you can find all the ingredients quickly, as may not be the case for those unfamiliar with crystallized ginger. Also known as candied ginger, it is ginger that has been saturated and coated with sugar. You can find it in most supermarket produce or spice sections.)

YIELDS 2 SERVINGS

Blend the cream cheese and ginger in a bowl with an electric mixer. Stir the grapes into the cream cheese mixture to coat: Chop the toasted almonds finely. Roll the grapes in the almonds. Place on a wax-paper lined plate. Chill until firm.

1 (3-ounce) package cream cheese, softened

1 tablespoon finely chopped crystallized ginger

15 to 20 seedless grapes, washed and thoroughly dried

1/2 cup almonds, toasted

champagne grape ring

sensual presentation

This recipe produces a glistening 3-dimensional portrait of plump grapes suspended in a translucent ring. And, as Jon so aptly reminds us, "Best part is you have to drink the remaining champagne so it doesn't go flat."

YIELDS 6 TO 8 SERVINGS

Boil 3/4 cup of water in a saucepan. Pour over the gelatin in a bowl and let set for 5 minutes to soften. Add the remaining 1/2 cup water along with the champagne; cool. Pour half the mixture in a 4-cup ring mold; allow to set. Arrange the grapes over the set gelatin. Pour the remaining gelatin mixture over top. Allow to set. Unmold before serving.

1 1/4 cups water, divided

1 (3-ounce) package orange gelatin

3/4 cup champagne

1 cup white seedless grapes

1 cup red seedless grapes

s t r a w b e r r i e s

In the words of one friend, "l'image que tu m'as envoyée a aiguisé mon goût pour . . . les fraises," which translates as, "the picture you sent me has raised my taste for . . . (delicious pause) . . . strawberries." • These fruits, rivaled only by the smooth cherry in innate sensuality, come as the harbinger of summertime. In the wild, the mix of tart and sweet red berries dot the landscape, swirling and twirling a thicket of glory. In the store, they come packed by the carton, shoppers peering carefully through each cellophane wrapper in hopes of finding the perfect, the red, the ultimate in strawberries. • Not a bad choice for an evening of seduction, the strawberry has a green button top that fits easily betwixt fingers. And more importantly, a berry that fits even more easily betwixt parted lips. • Imagine for just one moment your partner as a strawberry, lightly dusted with confectioners' sugar or slowly dipped in warm, creamy chocolate. Or just enjoy your lover as we most often do the strawberry — plain, and at its essence, beautifully ripe.

easy strawberry empanadas

creamy, sweet, and flaky all rolled into one

"Make sure you crimp the edges together well because there's no way you want to lose any of that warm creamy filling. We ate ours in the living room, feet up on the couch, with our favorite Nat King Cole songs playing in the background. Unforgettable." *Marilyn and Tom, married 26 years, Memphis, TN*

1/4 cup cream cheese

4 tablespoons light brown sugar, divided

2/3 cup coarsely chopped fresh strawberries

1 (8-count) package refrigerated crescent rolls

2 tablespoons butter, melted

YIELDS 4 EMPANADAS

Preheat oven to 350 degrees. Blend the cream cheese and 2 tablespoons brown sugar in a bowl. Fold in the strawberries. Unfold the crescent roll dough into 4 rectangles. Divide strawberry mixture among the 4 pieces, spooning onto bottom half of rectangle. Fold dough over and crimp edges. Bake rolls according to package directions until golden. Brush the cooked empanadas with melted butter, and dust with the remaining sugar before serving.

strawberry-avocado salad

a perfect summer salad

"Our first attempt at the strawberry-avocado salad ended in blissful failure. Wilted lettuce. Brown avocado. Burnt pecans. When we were asked by our over-eager friends the next day how everything went, we could only shrug — red stained fingers momentarily hiding our strawberry-swollen lips." *Sophie and Dustin, newlyweds, Atlanta, GA*

1/4 cup olive oil

1/4 cup raspberry vinegar

1 1/2 tablespoons sugar

1/4 teaspoon hot sauce

1/4 teaspoon salt

1/8 teaspoon pepper

1/4 teaspoon cinnamon

1 head romaine, torn into bite-size pieces

1/2 (11-ounce) can mandarin oranges, drained

1 cup strawberries, stemmed and quartered

1/2 cup sliced red onion (about 1/2 small onion)

1/4 cup coarsely chopped toasted pecans

1/2 avocado, sliced

YIELDS 2 TO 3 SERVINGS

Combine the olive oil, vinegar, sugar, hot sauce, salt, pepper, and cinnamon in a jar. Shake well and refrigerate for 2 hours.

Combine the romaine, oranges, strawberries, onion, pecans, and avocado in a large bowl. Top with half the dressing; toss well. Serve with the remaining dressing.

"My husband couldn't get enough of it! He liked the sauce too."

Diane in response to her husband's reaction to strawberry sauce served over grilled fish. Diane and Dave, married 4 years, Cincinnati, OH

lemon-pepper shrimp and strawberry salad

a spicy-sweet mingling

In the words of Carlene on this dish and her 50-year marriage to Turner, "Our relationship thrives on the delight we have enjoying such simple and beautiful things together."

YIELDS 2 TO 3 SERVINGS

Dressing:
- $1/2$ cup light vegetable oil
- 1 teaspoon lemon juice
- $1/2$ cup strawberries
  dash of lemon-pepper
  sugar, salt, and
  pepper to taste
- 2 teaspoons poppy seeds

Salad:
- 8 jumbo shrimp, shelled and deveined
  juice of $1/2$ lemon
- $3/4$ teaspoon lemon-pepper
- $2^1/2$ cups mixed greens, torn
- $1/2$ pint strawberries, halved

Combine the oil, 1 teaspoon lemon juice, $1/2$ cup strawberries, dash of lemon-pepper, sugar, salt, and pepper in a blender. Blend well, then add the poppy seeds. Sprinkle shrimp with juice of $1/2$ lemon, $3/4$ teaspoon lemon-pepper, and salt and pepper. Thread on skewers. Grill on a hot greased grill for 6 minutes or until firm to the touch and opaque throughout, turning once. Toss torn greens with vinaigrette to coat. Top with the shrimp and garnish with the strawberries and additional vinaigrette.

cornish hens
with strawberry glaze

beautiful presentation

To add a hint of exotica to the evening, Jim and Laurel suggest renaming the dish "Pornish

Game Hens." But they warn this recipe is not for the weak at heart — Jim prepared the dish

following a long day at work for the both of them and, as he sadly laments, the timing just

wasn't right for Pornish Game Hens: "After Laurel fought to get her food off that little hen, she

wasn't in the mood." Fortunately, he had some puréed strawberries left. Putting them to good

use, he spoonfed them to Laurel until she regained her strength and, once again, felt the full

effect of the strawberries on her libido.

YIELDS 2 SERVINGS

Combine the puréed strawberries, vinegar, lemon zest, shallot, mint, and ground pepper in a small bowl. Whisk in the olive oil until well blended. Marinate the Cornish hens in the strawberry mixture for 4 hours in the refrigerator.

Grill, skin side down, over a hot fire, basting frequently with the marinade. Turn after 10 minutes. Cook for 25 to 30 minutes or until juices run clear. Garnish if desired.

1/4 cup puréed strawberries
1/2 cup strawberry vinegar
zest of 1 lemon
2 teaspoons minced shallot
1 tablespoon minced mint
ground pepper to taste
2 tablespoons olive oil
2 Cornish hens, split
fresh strawberries and
mint leaves for garnish

white chocolate strawberry trifle

decadent layers

"I invited him over for dinner. I really didn't know what to expect. I wasn't feeling real sexy before he got there. I'm not the best cook in the world, so I was a little frantic trying to get everything to come out right. But I guess the planets were aligned correctly because everything was perfect. The entrée didn't burn, he showed up on time, a first, with flowers and bottle of wine in hand, and the white chocolate-strawberry trifle convinced him that he didn't need to leave quite as soon as he had planned." *Sarah, commenting on dessert and her 3-month dating relationship with Daniel, Jackson, MS*

YIELDS 4 TO 6 SERVINGS

1/3 cup sugar

2 egg yolks

3/4 teaspoon vanilla

1 (3-ounce) package cream cheese, softened

1/2 cup whipping cream

1 teaspoon instant espresso, dissolved in 1/2 cup hot water

4 ounces pound cake

3 ounces shaved white chocolate

3/4 cup sliced strawberries (about 1/2 pint)

Mix the sugar and egg yolks in a blender for 1 minute. Add the vanilla and blend 1 minute. Add the cream cheese and blend until smooth. Chill. Beat the whipping cream until stiff. Add the cream cheese mixture and chill. Slice cake into 1x3-inch strips. Dip the strips in hot espresso. Layer half the cake strips, white chocolate, cream cheese mixture, and strawberries in a clear bowl. Repeat layers. Cover and chill until ready to serve.

I break out in hives. It's not a food allergy. It's the pure excitement of the luscious scarlet fruit tempting my tongue. And his luscious tongue tempting my scarlet fruit.

Leila comments on her berry fetish.

chocolate cake dressed in berries

o h   b a b y

I knew that my husband had a business dinner that night. But I told him before he left that morning to save room for dessert when he came home. The anticipation was enough to drive me crazy. He got home around 8 o'clock. I left a note on the entrance hall table where he always stops and sets down his briefcase. The note instructed him to go into the dining room, where I left a second note on his plate with a blindfold. The note instructed him, "Put on the blindfold." He did, and then I walked into the room and said in a stern voice, "Are you ready for your just desserts?" He said, "Yes," a tinge of fearful excitement in his voice. "Okay, take off your blindfold," I said. He did and the look on his face was priceless. There I was, naked except for some strategically placed whipped cream and holding the chocolate cake dressed in berries. I asked, "You did leave room for dessert, didn't you?" He didn't answer, but I guess he did because he ate two desserts that night.

YIELDS 6 TO 8 SERVINGS

½ cup toasted almonds,
   finely chopped

3 tablespoons unsweetened
   cocoa powder

⅓ cup butter

½ cup sugar

2 tablespoons brown sugar

2 eggs

½ teaspoon vanilla

¼ cup chopped
   fresh strawberries

¼ cup strawberry preserves

2 tablespoons heavy cream

3 ounces semi-sweet
   chocolate chips
   strawberries for garnish

Combine the almonds and cocoa powder in a small bowl. Cream the butter and sugars in a bowl until fluffy. Beat in the eggs and the vanilla. Fold in the almond mixture, then the fresh strawberries. Spoon mixture into a greased 8-inch springform pan. Bake at 350 degrees for 35 to 45 minutes or until cake tests done. Cool completely. Remove from the pan. Spread with the strawberry preserves. Bring cream to a boil in a small saucepan. Remove from heat and add chocolate chips. Stir until smooth; cool for 5 minutes. Pour over top of cake (let drizzle down the sides). Garnish with fresh strawberries if desired.

strawberry pasta

not the traditional red sauce

"I have to admit to you that when Sharon told me she was going to make a meal for me that would curl my toes, I was thrilled. Sharon is a great cook who rarely has much time. When she told me that the main course was strawberry pasta, I was totally disappointed. I am a proud meat and potatoes kind of guy after all and strawberry pasta just sounded so . . . so . . . wimpy. But I kept all of this to myself — thank the culinary gods. Because that night Sharon found a way to make strawberries, cream, and noodles taste like ambrosia. She also found a way to curl my toes. I think my meat and potato days are over." *Jeremy on dining with his culinary goddess, friends 3 years, Biblically involved 4 months, Nacogdoches, TX*

YIELDS 2 TO 3 SERVINGS

Purée the strawberries in a blender. Strain to remove seeds. Cook the spaghetti using the package directions; drain and toss with the cheese. Heat the butter and cream in a small saucepan. Move the pasta to a serving bowl, cover with strawberries, and then the butter sauce. Toss well. Serve with additional cheese and garnish with mint, if desired.

1   pint fresh strawberries
½   pound spaghetti
¼   cup grated pecorino or
    Parmesan cheese
2   tablespoons butter
¼   cup heavy cream
    mint sprigs for garnish

honey

From the *Kama Sutra* to the *Perfumed Garden* to the *Bible*, honey has been connected with love, sex, and sensuality extraordinaire since the beginning of time. In the 5th century B.C., Hippocrates prescribed it for sexual vigor. Tradition in India offers a bridegroom honey on his wedding day. Newlyweds typically go on a honeymoon, a practice that stems from an ancient tradition of couples going into seclusion and drinking a honey concoction until the first new moon of their marriage. In fact, Attila the Hun drank himself to death with honey on his honeymoon.

• Physiologically, honey provides the body with a very usable form of sugar that converts easily into energy. Psychologically, honey encompasses sensuality. The very word honey conjures up golden images of the dripping, sticky, viscous substance, of honeybees, of honeysuckle, of all things sweet. And why shouldn't it? It comes from the nectar of flowers, from orange blossoms and dandelions, from raspberries and clover, from springtime and buzzing bees. Taste and enjoy.

honey-nut pie

richly flavored with citrus overtones

You are my honey, honeysuckle, I am the bee. When Randall saw this quote from Albert Fitz's 1901 song, he immediately thought of his grandparents, Valley and Lawrence. The story goes something like this: Lawrence and his brother, native Iowans, needed work and wives. They trekked around the country, doing odd jobs to support their main quest for love, until they came to a small town in Arkansas where Lawrence met Valley. He must have wooed her well, because she moved with him back to Iowa where they married and began their family. Lawrence made his living as a beekeeper, always supplying Valley with honey galore. Valley loved Lawrence, Lawrence loved Valley, the bees loved Lawrence (he never once received a sting), and they both loved honey. Valley and Lawrence lived a full marriage of 69 happy years, and Randall will always remember them for their honey-sweet love.

YIELDS 6 SERVINGS

1 cup honey

1½ cups chopped walnuts

2 teaspoons grated lemon peel

4 tablespoons dark rum

2 tablespoons dried bread crumbs

1 tablespoon sugar

2 (8-inch) frozen pie crusts, thawed

1 egg yolk

1 tablespoon milk

1½ cups whipped cream

Preheat the oven to 400 degrees. Heat the honey in a small saucepan. Add the walnuts and lemon peel. Simmer until the mixture is hot and the walnuts are well-coated with honey. Remove from the heat and stir in the rum; set aside. Spread the bread crumbs and sugar on the bottom of 1 pie crust. Spoon in the honey mixture. Top with the other pie crust. Seal the edges. Prick the top of the dough to let steam escape. Mix the egg yolk and milk in a small bowl. Brush over the top of the pie. Bake for 30 to 40 minutes or until the pastry is golden brown. Cool and serve with the whipped cream.

honey-almond delight

flaky niblets reminiscent of baklava

Mara has a crush on her Jeff. Jeff works for Mara. She's never played the secret admirer, but she thought now might be the perfect time to start. First tactic? Honey-almond delight in kraft paper packaging with no return address. He liked it — ate the whole package in 2 days — but doesn't seem to have a clue as to the identity of his admirer. Next tactic? Mara says she's thinking of inviting him over for *Star Wars* and pizza, but will accidentally rent *Sense and Sensibility*.

Mara and Jeff, not yet together, Arlington, VA

YIELDS 40 PIECES

Line a 15x10-inch jelly roll pan with foil.

Combine 1/2 pound butter, 1/2 cup sugar, salt, and almond extract; mix well. Add the egg and flour. Press the dough into the pan, pushing up the sides. Refrigerate for 1 hour. Prick dough with a fork. Bake at 375 degrees for 10 minutes. Combine the brown sugar, honey, and the remaining butter and sugar in a saucepan. Simmer until sugar dissolves, stirring occasionally. Bring to a boil. Cook for 3 minutes without stirring. Remove from heat and stir in the cream and almonds. Spread over the crust. Bake for 10 to 15 minutes more or until bubbly. Cool and cut into triangles.

1 pound butter, divided
3/4 cup sugar, divided
1/2 teaspoon salt
3/4 teaspoon almond extract
1 egg
2 3/4 cups flour
1 cup brown sugar
1/3 cup honey
1/4 cup heavy cream
1 pound sliced almonds (about 5 cups)

king solomon: Your lips drop sweetness as the honeycomb, my bride; milk and honey are under your tongue . . . You are a garden locked up . . . you are a spring enclosed, a sealed fountain . . . a well of flowing water streaming down from Lebanon.

lover: Awake, north wind, and come, south wind! Blow on my garden, that its fragrance may spread abroad. Let my lover come into his garden and taste its choice fruits.

king solomon: I have come into my garden . . . my bride; I have gathered my myrrh with my spice. I have eaten my honeycomb and my honey; I have drunk my wine and my milk.

god: Eat, O friends, and drink; drink your fill, O lovers.

french toast baked
in honey-pecan sauce

puffed clouds of ecstacy

This recipe offers the most ultimate experience in french toast. For delectable results, stray not from the recipe, preparing it the day ahead with thick slices of a baguette. The eggs and cream and sweeteners saturate the bread overnight, then puff up to a golden, sticky ecstasy in the morning's hot oven.

YIELDS 2 TO 3 SERVINGS

Combine the eggs, half-and-half, brown sugar, and vanilla extract in a small bowl. Pour half the mixture into a baking dish. Place the bread in the pan and top with other half of egg mixture. Refrigerate, covered, overnight.

Melt the butter in a 9x13-inch baking dish and stir in the brown sugar, honey, maple syrup, and pecans. Add the soaked bread slices. Bake at 350 degrees for 30 to 35 minutes until puffed and brown. Serve immediately.

4   eggs, beaten
3/4 cup half-and-half
1/2 tablespoon brown sugar
1   teaspoon vanilla extract
4   thick slices French bread
1/4 cup butter (1/2 stick)
1/4 cup brown sugar
1/4 cup honey
1/4 cup maple syrup
1/4 cup chopped pecans

For that extra something on your toast, make a batch of honey butter. It keeps up to 4 weeks and is simple to make. Just combine 1 stick butter, 2/3 cup honey, and 1/3 cup light brown sugar with an electric mixer or food processor. Store in a crock and chill until firm.

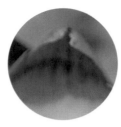

a r t i c h o k e s

Tough green leaves, each armed with its own thorn, stand on guard. They rally their strength to make one tightly woven bud, protecting the exquisite beauty found inside their walls. This aphrodisiac, like many lovers, plays hard to get (which, like many suitors, just makes one want it more). • Fortunately, some very hungry body figured out how to unleash the velvety softness found only in the stubborn artichoke. • Experience it for yourself: Together with your partner, insert your thumbs into the very center of a blanched artichoke, where the leaves meet. Slowly pull the petals apart and down. As the leaves fold down, they will reveal a veritable painting of green, white, and purple. Don't stop there, but delve deeper toward the center. Continue spreading the petals until you spy a hint of yellowy-white fur. Insert a finger into the opening. The fur, you will find, is protected by the prickly spears of the choke. But persevere, close your eyes, and stroke the voluptuous fur.

baked artichoke and crab dip

an elegant alternative to chips and queso

Serve this at a party where you're trying to play cupid. The artichoke should send all arrows straight to the heart, making things a bit easier on you.

YIELDS 2 TO 3 SERVINGS

1   small green bell
    pepper, chopped
½ tablespoon vegetable oil
1   (14-ounce) can artichoke
    hearts, drained and
    finely chopped
1   pickled jalapeño pepper,
    seeded and minced
1   cup mayonnaise
¼ cup thinly sliced scallions
¼ cup chopped pimento
½ cup grated Parmesan cheese
    juice of 1 small lemon
2   teaspoons Worcestershire
    sauce
½ teaspoon celery salt
½ pound crab meat
¼ cup toasted sliced almonds

Sauté the green pepper in oil in a small skillet until tender; drain. Combine with the artichokes, jalapeño, mayonnaise, scallions, pimento, Parmesan cheese, lemon juice, Worcestershire sauce, and celery salt in a large bowl. Fold in the crab meat. Place mixture in a greased baking dish. Sprinkle with the almonds. Bake at 375 degrees for 25 to 30 minutes or until golden brown and bubbly. Serve with pita crisps or salsa and tortilla chips.

bruschetta with purée of artichokes

unbelievable flavors

For someone who has never prepared an artichoke, the task can seem quite daunting. But don't let
it be. Here are the basics: Store the artichoke in a plastic bag in the coldest part of the refrigerator.
Don't cut an artichoke until you're ready to use it. It will turn brown almost immediately. (Rubbing
cut surfaces with lemon juice or storing the cut artichoke in lemon water helps stop discoloration.)
To get to the heart of the artichoke, cut off the stem. Snap off the tough outer leaves. Trim the spiny
tips off remaining leaves. Slice off the top third and the bottom inch of the artichoke. Remove any
of the spindly choke (a grapefruit spoon works nicely), as well as remaining green leaves. Rub with
lemon and store in lemon water until ready to use.

YIELDS 2 TO 3 SERVINGS

Sauté the garlic, salt, pepper, and artichokes in olive oil. Add about ½ cup of water and simmer, covered, until artichokes are tender. (Add water if needed.) Mash the ingredients to a coarse paste. Add the olives, tomato, parsley, and capers to the skillet. Just before serving, grill or toast the bread. Drizzle with olive oil, and top each slice with the artichoke mixture. Garnish with a leaf of parsley.

2   cloves garlic, crushed
    salt and pepper to taste
2   medium artichoke hearts
1½ tablespoons olive oil
5   oil-cured ripe olives, pitted
    and chopped
1   small tomato, seeded
    and chopped
2   tablespoons chopped
    Italian parsley
1   tablespoon capers
2   thick slices French or
    Italian bread
    extra-virgin olive oil
    additional parsley for
    garnish

artichoke and scallop kebabs

lowfat aphrodisia at its best

Be forewarned: this recipe contains multiple aphrodisiac ingredients. From the onion, garlic, and jalapeño to the artichokes and scallops, these skewers have the potential to wield power over all who indulge. As an aside, have you ever seen a scallop in its shell? Please make a point to do so. Sensual and absolutely magnificent.

YIELDS 2 SERVINGS

1 large tomato, minced
1 small onion, minced
1 clove garlic, minced
1 small jalapeño, seeded and minced
  juice of 1/2 a lime
3 sprigs cilantro, chopped
  pinch of sugar
  salt and pepper to taste
2 medium-size zucchini
1 (9-ounce) jar artichoke hearts
2 ounces fresh sea scallops or shrimp
2 teaspoons lime juice

Place the tomato, onion, garlic, and jalapeño in a small bowl. Add the juice of 1/2 lime, cilantro, sugar, salt, and pepper. Mix well and let flavors meld at room temperature for 1 hour before serving. (Salsa can be made up to 10 days in advance and stored in the refrigerator in a tightly covered container.) • If using wooden skewers, pre-soak in water for about 15 minutes.

Slice the zucchini into 1/2-inch rounds. Drain and quarter the artichokes, reserving the oil. Rinse the scallops. Alternate the zucchini, artichokes, and scallops on the skewers. Brush with the reserved oil and 2 teaspoons lime juice. Grill over hot coals for 6 to 8 minutes, turning occasionally, or until scallops are opaque. Serve with the salsa.

"As the skewer penetrated the goodies, Laurel became more involved with cooking than ever before. She couldn't stand it as I slowly, ritually skewered the plump scallops next to the slippery-slick hearts of the artichoke. And then—when it was her turn to skewer—wowza!"

Jim, in response to the experience of preparing artichoke and scallop kebabs with Laurel, married 28 years, Houston, TX

artichoke muffaletta

easy twist on a new orleans' classic

For a subliminally sexy sandwich, Jen and Henry recommend replacing the securing toothpicks with butcher's twine and tying up the muff. Get it really hot in a 350 degree oven. Remove the steaming, aromatic muff of melded spices drenched in melting cheese, then just dive in. Sure beats eating out, no?

½ cup pesto

1 teaspoon Dijon mustard

½ loaf crusty French bread

1 cup artichoke hearts, thinly sliced

2 ounces provolone cheese, thinly sliced

1 small tomato, thinly sliced

1 cup (about 2 ounces) fresh spinach leaves

YIELDS 2 SERVINGS

Combine the pesto and mustard in a small bowl; mix well. Cut the bread in half lengthwise. Hollow out the top half, leaving a 1-inch shell. (Dip the insides in the pesto, and eat on the spot.) Spread the pesto mixture over each half. On one half, layer artichokes, cheese, tomato, and spinach. Top with the other half. Cut crosswise into 3 or 4 pieces; secure with wooden picks.

artichoke potato salad

gourmet picnic fare

Thinking about packing a picnic? Give this simple recipe to your sweetie and fill your picnic basket with fresh fruit, deli ham and cheese, a bottle of wine, a book of poetry (try *American Primitive* by Mary Oliver), a blanket, and all those extras that make a day in the park a day to be remembered.

1 pound unpeeled small new potatoes, scrubbed

¼ cup mayonnaise

½ tablespoon red wine vinegar

½ tablespoon Dijon mustard lemon-pepper to taste

1 teaspoon dill

1 hard-cooked egg, chopped

½ (9-ounce) jar marinated artichoke hearts, drained and chopped

3 tablespoons chopped onion

½ tablespoon chopped dill pickle

YIELDS 2 TO 3 SERVINGS

Cook the potatoes in water in a covered saucepan for 20 minutes or until tender; drain. Cut into bite-size pieces. Combine the mayonnaise, vinegar, mustard, lemon-pepper seasoning, and dill in a large bowl. Add the egg and artichokes to the mayonnaise mixture. Fold in the potatoes, onion, and pickle. Chill, covered, for 24 hours.

artichoke pizza with feta and thyme

hummus-like purée makes this pizza unique

For my friends and me, pizza has become our staple of choice for rented movies. Popcorn when you pay; pizza when you rent. Pick the right movie (*Moonstruck* or *Bull Durham*, perhaps?), the right person, and most certainly, you'll see that you have a pizza that can take things to the next level.

YIELDS 2 TO 3 SERVINGS

Heat the oil in a skillet. Add the bell peppers. Sauté for 3 minutes. Add half the garlic. Sauté until tender; set aside. Combine the remaining garlic, mayonnaise, crushed red pepper, black pepper, and artichoke hearts in a food processor. Process until finely chopped. Place the pizza crust on a baking sheet. Top with the artichoke mixture then the bell pepper mixture. Sprinkle with the cheeses and thyme. Bake at 450 degrees for about 15 minutes.

1   teaspoon olive oil
1   small red bell pepper, chopped
½   small yellow or orange bell pepper, chopped
2   garlic cloves, crushed
¼   cup mayonnaise
¼   teaspoon crushed red pepper
⅛   teaspoon black pepper
1   (9-ounce) can artichoke hearts, drained
1   (1-pound) cheese-flavored pizza crust
½   cup (2-ounces) crumbled feta cheese
½   cup Parmesan cheese
½   teaspoon dried thyme

black beans

It was around 400 A.D. when Saint Jerome, a Father of the Latin Church, first told his nuns "No." No, that is, to black beans. No touching, no eating, no puréeing, no refrying them. Well, perhaps his edict was not that restricting. But he did get his point across — for a nun avowed to celibacy, black beans were bad news. • Maybe that's what Sister Agnes ate. You see, black beans have put in many hours towards procreation. Lore has it that they increase fertility. It all starts with the fresh bean pod. Nestled in its protective casing, the black bean rests like a child in its mother. Then, when it is time, it emerges a smooth, blue-black color of midnight. Cleansed in water, it turns a magnificently shiny black, smooth like a pebble washed down from years of wear. Once cooked, the bean becomes a plump, yet firm signal to a woman's lips, heart, womb, that she is prepared to become with child. And so the cycle continues, creating love and children everywhere

sweet bean pudding

exotic breakfast or dessert option

A dear friend of mine lost her first baby during her eighth month of pregnancy. After 2 years of trying, she finally conceived again. In her eighth month of pregnancy, she agreed to pose for the black bean image, to symbolize its aphrodisiac quality of fertility and healing for women. On June 12, 1996, she gave birth to the most beautiful baby boy the world has ever seen. He weighed 8 pounds, 12 ounces, and he's just as sweet as this sweet bean pudding.

YIELDS 5 SERVINGS

1 cup cooked black beans

1 teaspoon grated orange zest

1/3 cup plus 1 tablespoon sugar

1 (14-ounce) can pure coconut milk

2 tablespoons water
pinch of salt

3/4 cup short-grain white, Jasmine, or Arborio rice

1/2 teaspoon vanilla extract

6 banana leaves (or 12 tamale husks)

1 ripe banana, sliced in rounds

Mash the beans with orange zest and 1 tablespoon of the sugar in a small bowl; set aside. Combine the coconut milk, water, sugar, and salt in a medium saucepan. Bring to a boil. Add the rice and reduce heat to medium. Cook for 12 minutes or until the milk is absorbed and the rice half cooked, stirring frequently. • Remove from heat, stir in vanilla, and allow to cool. Tear 1 banana leaf into 4 strips to use as "ties"; set aside. Place another leaf on the work surface. Spoon 3 tablespoons of the rice mixture in center. Place 3 tablespoons beans over the rice. Place 3 rounds of banana on the beans, and top with another 2 tablespoons of rice. Fold the banana leaf around the mixture like an eggroll. Tie a banana leaf strip around the package for stability, then repeat the process for the remaining packets. Boil water in a steamer pot. Add the packets to the steamer rack over the boiling water. Steam, covered, for 45 minutes or until rice is tender; cool. Serve in packets, as you would homemade tamales.

" He made me a margarita, fluffed up my favorite chair, put on some Ruben Blades, and brought over a bowl of black bean salsa and chips. That's why I love him. "

Amy on her husband Steve who still, after 11 years of marriage, manages to surprise her with his kind heart.

black bean salsa

Carlene and Turner, together 50 years come March and parents of an unbelievable daughter named Martha, describe this salsa as "a very satisfying dish with a definite exotic flavor." • I never like to hear of my parents' love life. (Parents, as we all know, do not have sex. Especially ones who were missionaries for 10 years.) But the following description was tame enough to keep me from wincing. Says Carlene, "It brought to mind Caribbean beaches and a romantic dinner for two under the swaying palm trees. This added romantic excitement to the evening." My father reinforced her quote with a grin and a wink.

1 ripe mango,
   peeled and diced
¼ red bell pepper, diced
¼ green bell pepper, diced
¼ red onion, diced
½ cup canned black beans
⅓ cup pineapple juice
   juice of 2 limes
¼ cup chopped cilantro
1 tablespoon ground cumin
½ tablespoon minced
   green chile pepper
   salt and pepper to taste

YIELDS 2 TO 3 SERVINGS

Combine the mango, peppers, onion, black beans, juices, cilantro, cumin, and chile pepper in a bowl. Season with salt and pepper. Chill, covered, for up to 5 days. Serve as a snack with tortilla chips or, better yet, fried plantain rounds.

black bean fritters

I first made this dish for a co-ed bridal shower/bon voyage gift to a co-worker who would be traveling to Greece with her fiancé and 3-carat diamond for a wedding on the beach in Cyros. All in attendance oohed and ahhed over these fritters drizzled in an almost-drinkable vinaigrette, and the couple is still married. Must be the beans.

½ red bell pepper, diced
½ yellow bell pepper, diced
½ chayote or zucchini, diced
1 cup cooked black beans
½ cup cornmeal
½ cup flour
½ tablespoon baking powder
1 tablespoon packed
   brown sugar
1 egg
2 tablespoons buttermilk
   salt and pepper to taste
   peanut oil for frying

YIELDS 2 TO 3 SERVINGS

Combine the bell peppers, chayote, black beans, cornmeal, flour, baking powder, and brown sugar in a large bowl. Add the egg and buttermilk and toss lightly. Season with salt and pepper. Heat the peanut oil in a heavy saucepan to 350 degrees. Drop the black bean mixture into the oil by spoonfuls. Fry 3 to 5 minutes or until thoroughly cooked. Serve with *tropical vinaigrette*.

tropical vinaigrette

smooth and delicious

This recipe creates more than enough vinaigrette for the fritters. But by all means, do not throw the leftover away. Save and serve later over fruit salad, grilled chicken, or, god forbid, iceberg lettuce.

Blend the mango and passion fruit juice in a blender. Combine the vinegar and lime juice in a small bowl. Add vinegar mixture and peanut oil to the mango while the blender is slowly running. Mix in orange juice, salt, and honey. Store, refrigerated, in an airtight container.

1 mango, peeled with seed removed (the mango seed: another fun play toy for couples)
½ cup passion fruit juice
½ cup rice wine vinegar
3 tablespoons lime juice
1 cup peanut oil
2 tablespoons orange juice
  salt to taste
  honey to taste

black bean chili

for wintertime warmth

As with all great chilis of the world, this one is better on day two. It's perfect, then, for those nights when you want to devote more time to thinking about which boots you want to wear with your jeans than how to best mince a clove of garlic. (Oh, by the way, don't flinch at the abundance of onions and garlic. While not officially covered in this cookbook, they are both well-regarded aphrodisiacs according to many. And besides, if both of you smell like garlic and onions, then who will be bothered?)

Brown the ground chuck and chorizo in a skillet; drain. Rinse and drain the soaked beans. Combine the beans and water in a large pot. Bring to a boil over medium heat. Add the red pepper, onion, celery, tomatoes, carrot, garlic, vinegar, beer, cayenne pepper, and chiles to the beans. Simmer, covered, for 1½ hours or until beans are tender. Add the ground chuck and chorizo sausage. Simmer, covered, for 1 hour more. Garnish with scallions and sour cream. Serve with rice, crumbled corn bread, or tortilla chips.

½ pound ground chuck
½ pound chorizo sausage, cut up
1 cup dried black beans, soaked overnight
3 cups water
1 small red bell pepper or ½ a medium, chopped
1 medium onion, chopped
1 rib celery, chopped
2 tomatoes, peeled and chopped
1 medium carrot, chopped
1 tablespoon minced garlic
2 tablespoons white wine vinegar
½ cup beer
½ teaspoon cayenne pepper
2 tablespoons ground chiles or to taste
  chopped scallions and sour cream for garnish

o y s t e r s

Perhaps the greatest of all aphrodisiacs, the oyster symbolizes virility and passion for all who indulge. From Petronius to Casanova, oysters have unleashed their powers of seduction on unwitting prey and restored life to lagging libidos. • The oyster's powers are best experienced when eaten on the half shell. In this state, the oyster is most reminiscent of key body parts, officially qualifying it as an aphrodisiac. Some see the closed shell as the male testes, while others see the fresh oyster itself as better representation. But few can debate the beauty (or implications) of the oyster resting in its half shell, nether petals of pink and gray fluttering out from the meat onto a pearly white backdrop. • If the sheer visual effects of the oyster do not suffice, then consider the oyster's nutritional benefits to the human body: they are low in fat, high in complex sugars and proteins. More importantly, though, oysters are loaded with zinc, a key ingredient to testosterone production and, hence, sexual performance for both genders.

grilled oysters

the next best alternative to raw

Oyster aficionados Marie and Richard tested this recipe too, reaffirming in the process the oyster's aphrodisiac power over them: "Oysters take us back to our honeymoon in New Orleans when we consumed about 3 to 4 dozen a day. Perhaps that memory contributed to the fun we had now, three years later, grilling oysters together and eating them in our make-do, candle-lit picnic in the living room floor."

YIELDS 2 SERVINGS

1 dozen oysters in the shell
3/4 cup bread crumbs
3 tablespoons finely chopped parsley
1 clove garlic, crushed
juice of 1/2 lemon
olive oil to taste
salt and pepper to taste

Remove the top shell of the oysters, being careful to not lose the liquor. (It will make a nice juice for the oysters to simmer in.) Combine the bread crumbs, parsley, and garlic in a small bowl. Spoon on each oyster. Sprinkle with lemon juice, olive oil, salt, and pepper.

Grill for 12 minutes or until the bread crumbs are golden. For a simpler version, simply clean the oysters, place on medium-hot grill, and remove when they begin to open.

Shuck, squeeze with lemon, et voilà.

oysters on the half shell

the quintessential staple of aphrodisiac foods

Shucking can be fun (with protective gloves and an oyster knife, that is.) First, scrub and rinse the oysters thoroughly in cold water to prevent grit from invading the succulent morsel you're working so hard to get to. Next, work the knife into the slit near the "hinge" of the shell. Twist the knife forcefully until the shell begins to pop open. Work the knife around the rest of the shell to open completely.

YIELDS 2 SERVINGS

Combine the ketchup, horseradish, lemon juice, and Tabasco. Serve as a side to oysters on the half shell.

Cocktail Sauce
1 cup high-quality ketchup
¼ cup horseradish sauce
juice of 2 lemons
dash of Tabasco

baked oysters with chardonnay

delicate bites of oyster coated in warm cream

"Making this dish reminded us of our honeymoon 29 years ago in Cape Cod. We ate tons of oysters in many different dishes on that beautiful paradise by the ocean. What oysters did for us then, they still do for us today (maybe it's just the memories). Whatever the case, we believe it is romance in the form of food. Use wisely, and only with those who deserve it." *Matt and Carol, married 29 years, Philadelphia, PA*

YIELDS 2 SERVINGS

Drain the oysters, reserving the juice. Sauté the shallot in butter in a skillet for 1 minute to soften. Add the wine. Bring to a boil. Reduce the heat and simmer for 6 to 8 minutes or until the liquid is reduced by half. Add the reserved oyster juice. Cook for 2 minutes. Strain into a saucepan, discarding solids. Stir in the cream. Bring to a boil. Reduce the heat and simmer for 10 to 12 minutes or until the liquid is reduced by half. (Thicken with flour-water mixture if necessary.) Stir in the curry and salt. Arrange the oysters (in shells) in a roasting pan. Season with pepper and 1 tablespoon of sauce each. Bake at 450 degrees for 3 to 4 minutes or until the oysters are cooked and the cream is beginning to brown. Garnish with watercress.

24 oysters on the half shell
2 shallots, minced
1 tablespoon unsalted butter
1 cup Chardonnay or other dry white wine
1 cup heavy cream
1 teaspoon Madras curry
salt and pepper to taste

After they had swallowed a few oysters and drank one or two glasses of punch, which they liked amazingly, I begged Emilie to give me an oyster with her lips . . . I placed the shell on the edge of her lips, and after a good deal of laughing, she sucked in the oyster, which she held between her lips. I instantly recovered it by placing my lips on hers . . . My agreeable surprise may be imagined when I heard her say that it was my turn to hold the oysters. It is needless to say that I acquitted myself of the duty with much delight . . . [later] I scolded Armelline for having swallowed the liquid as I was taking the oyster from her lips. I agreed that it was very hard to avoid doing so, but offered to (show) them how it could be done by placing the tongue in the way. This gave me an opportunity of teaching them the game of tongues, which I shall not explain because it is well known to all true lovers . . . It so chanced that a fine oyster slipped from its shell as I was placing it between Emilie's lips. It fell onto her breast, and she would have recovered it with her fingers; but I claimed the right of regaining it myself. I got hold of the oyster with my lips, but did so in such a manner to prevent her suspecting that I had taken any extraordinary pleasure in the act.

Casanova, Memoirs, Volume 6,
Translated by Vera Lee in Secrets of Venus

parmesan cheese oysters

the jalapeños just keep things hot

Marie and Richard tested all three cheese oysters. Each recipe received high marks, but in the words of Marie herself . . . "We made about 15 oysters with the various toppings, but then started eating the remaining on the half shell — raw oysters are so sensual. As you eat it, if you chew a little, but then suck the raw oyster down, it can be very orally stimulating."

YIELDS 8 OYSTERS

Mix the bacon bits, onions, peppers, Parmesan cheese, and ½ cup bread crumbs in a small bowl; set aside. Arrange oyster shell halves (with oyster attached) on a baking sheet. Top 8 oysters with the Parmesan mixture. Bake at 350 degrees for 12 minutes.

¼ cup bacon bits
¼ cup chopped onion (about ½ small onion)
¼ cup chopped red and green bell peppers (about ½ small pepper)
¼ cup finely chopped jalapeño pepper
¼ cup grated Parmesan cheese
½ cup seasoned bread crumbs
2 tablespoons butter, softened
8 shucked oysters, on the half shell

cheddar cheese oysters

artichoke hearts add another layer of flavor

YIELDS 8 OYSTERS

Mix the artichokes, Cheddar cheese, vinaigrette, and bread crumbs in a small bowl; set aside. Arrange oyster shell halves (with oyster attached) on a baking sheet. Top 8 oysters with the artichoke mixture. Bake at 350 degrees for 12 minutes.

¼ cup chopped artichoke hearts
¼ cup shredded Cheddar cheese (about ⅛ pound)
2 tablespoons white wine vinaigrette dressing
¼ cup seasoned bread crumbs
8 shucked oysters, on the half shell

blue cheese oysters

the pungent cheese intensifies these oysters

YIELDS 8 OYSTERS

Mix the blue cheese, garlic, bread crumbs, and butter in a small bowl; set aside. Arrange oyster shell halves (with oyster attached) on a baking sheet. Top 8 oysters with the blue cheese mixture. Bake at 350 degrees for 12 minutes.

½ cup crumbled blue cheese
1 teaspoon chopped garlic
¼ cup seasoned bread crumbs
2 tablespoons butter, softened
8 shucked oysters, on the half shell

r o s e m a r y

Unmistakable. The scent of rosemary fills a room, consumes the olfactory. Whether growing in a sunlit window planter, flavoring olive oil and hot country bread, or scenting the soft curve of a woman's neck, rosemary entices the sense of smell. • Madame de Sévigné found rosemary intoxicating. Medieval women scented bath water with it to allure men. Perfumeries have incorporated its captivating scent into many a perfume formula. • Apparently it plays on humans' keen "scent memory" — our "strongest tie to most emotional experiences," according to Cynthia Watson in *Love Potions*. In theory, if the scent of rosemary is present during a particularly amorous event, future hints of rosemary's heady bouquet will hearken one's lover back to the pleasing affair. If executed properly, one may eventually evoke a Pavlovian "call to love" with a mere waft of it in the air. • But rosemary's charm does not stop with its fragrance: one should not ignore its tactile aphrodisiac properties. The soft needles on a sprig of rosemary tickle every nerve ending they brush past. All to say, rosemary is one very potent herb.

capellini with rosemary

balsamic vinegar adds a subtle zip

According to Dan of Sioux City, Iowa, "At the very least, this recipe made me look like I know how to cook. She got all impressed that I was using fresh herbs — whatever it takes, you know. I casually left some well-chosen poetry books next to the couch. (It's one of those chair-and-a-half couches. Another smart purchase on my part.) And while I have no definite proof of the correlation between rosemary and what happened later on, I am forever indebted to capellini with rosemary, Norton and his anthologies, and that too-small couch."

YIELDS 2 TO 3 SERVINGS

4 cloves garlic, minced

¼ cup plus 1 tablespoon olive oil

½ cup chopped rosemary

½ cup chopped parsley

½ cup chopped chives

1 pound (about 3 medium) tomatoes, diced

1 tablespoon balsamic vinegar

1 pound capellini

salt and pepper to taste

Heat three-fourths of the garlic in ¼ cup of the olive oil in a skillet until fragrant. Stir in the herbs and remove from the heat. Combine the tomatoes with the remaining garlic, 1 tablespoon olive oil, and vinegar in a small bowl. Set aside to marinate. Cook the pasta until al dente. Drain and toss with the herb mixture. Serve with the tomato mixture.

rosemary-scented lamb over pasta

satisfyingly rich

During my summer in Paris, I met a Lebanese man named Kamal. Toward the end of my stay, he

invited me over for dinner. Being the naive 19 year old that I was, I met him at his house for

8:00 dinner. A complete gentleman the whole evening, he showed me around his cracker-box

apartment and told me about his life as an officer in the Lebanese army. He showed me pictures

of his palatial estate in Lebanon. And then he showed the after-pictures of rubble, the war scars

on his back, and the letters from family he had to leave behind. He made me lamb and pasta that

night; we ate in his kitchen on a make-shift table with daisies he'd picked from his window box.

I never saw him again.

YIELDS 2 TO 3 SERVINGS

Sauté the garlic, lamb, and bell pepper until the lamb is tender. Over high heat, deglaze the pan with the wine, cooking until the liquid is almost evaporated. Add the tomato and rosemary. Simmer for 15 minutes. Stir in the cream, salt, and pepper. Cook until heated through. Toss with the warm rigatoni. Garnish with the cheese, rosemary, sage, and oregano. Serve immediately.

2   cloves garlic, chopped
5   ounces lamb, cut into
    thin strips
1/2 yellow or red bell pepper,
    cut into strips
1/4 cup dry white wine or
    chicken stock
1 1/2 cups crushed tomatoes
    sprig of rosemary
2   tablespoons heavy cream
    salt and pepper to taste
1/2 pound rigatoni, cooked
1/4 cup Parmesan cheese
1   teaspoon chopped rosemary
1   teaspoon chopped sage
1   teaspoon chopped oregano

herbed risotto

a chewy, delicately-scented dish

This risotto reminds me of my first experience with the creamy wonder: It was a late-night dinner following *City of Angels*. My date and I had wandered down one too many dark alleys when we stumbled upon a 5-table trattoria nestled between two closed shops. The only thing they had left to serve was their Thursday special — mushroom risotto. Try this recipe with some wine, bread, and candlelight. It worked for us.

YIELDS 2 TO 3 SERVINGS

1 ½ tablespoons unsalted butter
1 small onion, diced
¾ cup Arborio rice
2 cups hot chicken stock
  salt and pepper to taste
1 pound mushrooms, sliced
½ tablespoon olive oil
1 large ripe tomato, diced
¼ cup heavy cream
⅛ cup chopped basil
1 tablespoon minced
  fresh rosemary
1 tablespoon grated
  Parmesan cheese

Melt the butter in a large skillet. Sauté the onion until tender. Add the rice. Cook for 1 minute, stirring constantly. Add the chicken stock, salt, and pepper. Cook, covered until the rice is tender on the outside and chewy inside. While the rice is cooking, sauté the mushrooms in olive oil. When the rice is done, fold in the mushrooms, tomatoes, cream, basil, rosemary, and cheese.

FRESH ROSEMARY IS NOT SOMETHING THAT I NORMALLY

INCLUDE ON MY GROCERY LISTS. HONESTLY, I DIDN'T

EVEN KNOW WHERE TO FIND IT. SO WHEN I BEGAN

CHOPPING UP THIS HERB AND ITS PINEY SCENT FILLED MY

KITCHEN SPACE, I WAS SLIGHTLY AMAZED. ITS PRICKLY

NEEDLES SMELLED SO WARM AND OUTDOORSY. LIKE BEN.

BEN IS ALL LEATHER AND FLANNEL. ALL ROBERT REDFORD

AND PAUL BUNYAN. ALL-FOR-ONE AND ALL-AMERICAN.

AND ALTHOUGH YOU'D NEVER GET HIM TO ADMIT IT

— BEN IS TOTALLY *rosemary*.

Leanne's response to a dinner
of *pasta with rosemary cream
sauce* and Ben, her beau of
2 years, Fayetteville, AR

pasta with rosemary cream sauce

a classic

According to Josephine Addison's book on love potions, rosemary holds the key to a young girl's dreams of her husband-to-be. On St. Agnes Eve (January 21), she should sleep with rosemary beneath her pillow to see who he will be. For an engaged or married couple, rosemary symbolizes remembrance and fidelity, a definite turn-on for lovers everywhere. So make your wish, dream your dream, and then use your enchanted sprig of rosemary to prepare this simple and delectable dish.

YIELDS 2 TO 3 SERVINGS

½ pound penne pasta
⅛ cup fresh rosemary, minced
2 tablespoons olive oil
¾ cup tomato purée
   salt and pepper to taste
¼ cup heavy cream
¼ cup Parmesan cheese

Cook the penne in water until al dente. In the meantime, sauté the rosemary in the oil in a saucepan over low heat for 3 minutes. Add the tomato purée. Season with salt and pepper.

Simmer for 15 minutes. Pour in the cream and Parmesan, stirring until heated through. Drain pasta and toss with cream sauce.

rosemary cheese grits casserole

for grits-lovers everywhere

For those of you who have never tried grits, now is the time. Unbeknownst to most, grits are basically ground-up dried kernels of corn — nothing to be afraid of at all. This casserole puts a grown-up spin on traditional Southern grits for an oh-so-good combination of basic Italian ingredients.

YIELDS 2 TO 3 SERVINGS

Combine the olive oil, tomato purée, tomatoes, and garlic in a bowl. Layer the *grits cakes*, tomato mixture, fontina, and rosemary half at a time in a greased square baking dish. Top with Parmesan cheese. Bake for 30 to 40 minutes.

3 tablespoons olive oil
2 cups tomato purée
1 cup diced fresh tomatoes
4 cloves garlic, chopped
  grits cakes (see recipe below)
8 ounces fontina or mozzarella, shredded
2 tablespoons chopped fresh rosemary
  grated Parmesan

grits cakes

like potato cakes, only better

YIELDS 2 TO 3 SERVINGS

Prepare the grits according to package directions. Combine 1 of the eggs and the cream in a bowl; mix well. Quickly add some grits to the egg mixture, beating well with a wire whisk to incorporate. Stir mixture back into the remaining grits and whisk together well. Pour into a small greased casserole dish, then refrigerate until firm. Turn out onto a cutting surface, and cut into manageable rectangles. Beat the remaining egg with the 2 teaspoons of water in a bowl. Dip each wedge in the egg mixture, then dip in the meal. Sauté until golden brown in oil in a skillet; drain and keep warm.

1 cup instant grits
2 eggs
2 tablespoons heavy cream
2 teaspoons water
1/4 cup cornmeal
  peanut oil for frying

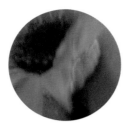

edible flowers

nasturtiums fuchsia lilies hibiscus roses orange blossoms jasmine chrysanthemums gladiolus orchids pansies lilacs apple borage lavender lemon violas marigolds geraniums daisies squash blossoms mimosas violets chamomile • "Flowers are the plants' sex organs, and they evoke the sex-drenched, bud-breaking free-for-all of spring and summer." An explanation of the aphrodisiacal power of flowers as only Diane Ackerman can say it. A *Natural History of Love*. • Lore has it that the sweet juice of the honey-suckle induces erotic dreams. Plucked off, one by one, daisy petals tell whether he loves me, or he loves me not. A dandelion, with one swift puff of air, tells of a lover's faithfulness (or lack of) to a relationship. • Flowers speak when people can't: The red velvet rose of love. The virgin white rose of purity. The unopened buds of innocence. A suitable variation exists for every conceivable situation, and from the carefree wildness of violets and hibiscus to the exquisite architecture of a single orchid, flowers run the gamut of the emotional mind and palate. Add them to your vocabulary.

sweet frittata with flowers

breakfast-in-bed fare

Those of you unfamiliar with frittatas, have no fear — a frittata is just an omelet in more elegant clothing. Omelets are fluffy semicircles with the ingredients folded inside. Frittatas, on the other hand, have the ingredients blended into the eggs first. And because they are cooked over lower heat for a longer length of time, frittatas tend to be a bit firmer and more well-done than their omelet cousins.

YIELDS 2 SERVINGS

4 eggs
½ cup edible flowers
(see list on page 92)
1 tablespoon cream
2 tablespoons cinnamon-sugar
1 tablespoon unsalted butter
confectioners' sugar
and additional flowers
for garnish

Preheat oven to 350 degrees. Beat eggs lightly in a bowl. Stir in the flowers, cream, and cinnamon. Melt the butter in a small ovenproof skillet. Add the egg mixture. Cook over low heat until the eggs form large curds, stirring constantly. Cook, without stirring, until the frittata is firm except for the top. Place skillet in the top third of the oven. Bake 2 to 4 minutes or until golden; cool in the pan for 1 to 2 minutes. Place a plate over top of skillet and invert the frittata. Sprinkle with confectioner's sugar and garnish with additional flowers if desired.

• **Flower Alert:** When cooking with flowers, make sure they are edible. First, choose an edible variety such as one listed on page 92. Then, purchase (or pick!) only unsprayed flowers since pesticides add an unruly, not to mention poisonous, flavor to dishes.

ravioli of fresh flowers

delicately translucent

"As the grand chef, I went into the yard to harvest squash blossoms and marigolds for our ravioli of fresh flowers. Since we grew them ourselves, we felt a real sense of accomplishment. As for the wonton skins, they have, in our experience, an intriguing texture that could cause one's mind to wander. Just toss the ravioli with some good pepper and fresh Parmesan to bring everything back into focus."

Charles on ravioli of fresh flowers and his own little flower Carla, married 42 years, Little Rock, AR

YIELDS 2 SERVINGS

Roll the wrappers into 4-inch squares. Brush *very lightly* with the cornstarch and water mixture.

Arrange herbs or blossoms on one diagonal of each square, leaving a 1/4-inch border. Fold the other half over to form a triangle. Press firmly to seal, forcing out as much air as possible. Trim edges with a pastry wheel if desired. Boil chicken stock in a large pot. Drop in 12 triangles. Boil for 3 minutes. Lift out with a skimmer and coat with half the melted butter. Repeat with the remaining triangles. Salt and pepper to taste. Serve with grated cheese as a light side dish.

24 wonton wrappers
cornstarch and water mixture
fresh blossoms (see list on page 92)
chicken stock for cooking pasta
1 tablespoon melted butter, divided
salt and pepper to taste
grated Parmesan cheese

"He kissed me under the Moorish wall and I thought well as well him as another and then I asked him with my eyes to ask again *yes* and then he asked me would I *yes* to say *yes* my mountain flower and first I put my arms around him *yes* and drew him down to me as he could feel my breasts all perfume *yes* and his heart was going like mad and *yes* I said *yes* I will *Yes*."

James Joyce, *Ulysses* (1922)

petals in white chocolate

vibrant colors captured on white

"To be honest, I had been seeing Jessica for a while and was ready for a little more, if you know what I mean. A friend of mine suggested I make her dinner, followed by a dessert bouquet of petals in white chocolate. During the course of the evening, I managed to spill wine on my carefully-chosen shirt, kitchen heat flattened my much worked-on hair, and the chicken tasted rubbery. Thankfully, Jessica was so moved by my efforts and the sweet little candies I made that she forgave the mishaps of earlier and gave me some sweet little candies of her own." *John on impressing Jessica, 3rd week of dating, Boston, MA*

YIELDS 10 CANDIES

Trim blossoms from the flowers and arrange 1 to 4 petals (depending on size) in each bonbon cup. Blossoms must lie as flat as possible. Melt the chocolate in a double boiler over hot, not boiling, water or microwave until melted, stirring frequently. Stir until smooth. Carefully fill each cup halfway with the melted chocolate. Chill, covered, for up to 4 hours. Peel off cups and arrange on a serving plate to showcase the petals.

edible blossoms such as unsprayed begonias, geraniums, lilacs, daisies, Johnny jump-ups, pansies, honeysuckle, roses, tulips, borage, lavender, violets, and pinks

10 bonbon cups

3 ounces sweet white chocolate, coarsely chopped

hibiscus cooler

utterly refreshing

Says Richard on this summer spritzer, "I was suddenly seized with a desire to shuffle." His wife, Marie, was suddenly seized with a desire to smile.

YIELDS 4 SERVINGS

Boil the water. Add the flowers and return water to a boil. Simmer for 5 to 10 minutes. Stir in the essential oil and sugar. Strain into a pitcher and chill. Serve over ice with orange slices and fresh edible petals.

1 quart water

1/2 cup dried hibiscus or other edible flowers

2 drops essential oil of orange

1/4 cup sugar or honey orange slices for garnish

p i n e   n u t s

Reatimus used them on the Romans. Galen, a 2nd century Greek doctor, prescribed them to his patients for their reported powers. Now, as we're approaching a new millennium, people are using the internet to hail the pine nut as one very deft kernel of love. • Pine nuts, also called pignolis, come from inside the cones of pine trees. This delicate and buttery nut, obtained with quite a struggle by heating the cone, comes in several varieties: Europeans eat an Italian or Swiss version; Asians use the strongly-flavored Chinese nut; Americans eat a Mexican nut. • But it is the communities around the northwestern Himalayas who rejoice the most. Privy to the pignoli of pignolis, a product of the Chilgoza Pine, they enjoy an outstanding birthrate. Perhaps pine nuts increase fertility. Or maybe they just increase copulation. Whatever the case, they're worth a try.

pine nut pie

a twist on grandmother's chess pie

"It was my third date with Josie. There had been sparks between us, but the circumstances hadn't allowed us to act on them the first two times. (At least, that was my read on the whole thing.) This time, I was cooking her dinner at my apartment, so I knew if anything was going to happen between us, this was it. She came over a little early, so I gave her a glass of wine and told her to make herself at home. She asked if she could play a CD. I told her sure, whatever she wanted to hear. She picked the Cowboy Junkies. In my mind, I was going 'Yes!' Then she came in the kitchen and sat on the counter. I'd just pulled the pie out the oven. She commented on how good it smelled, so I offered her a bite. I cut a little wedge and put it on a fork and started to hand it to her, warning her that it was hot. She then grabbed my hand with the fork in it and proceeded to blow on the food, her eyes never leaving me the whole time. I thought I was going to die. I cut off another piece. This time, she grabbed the fork out of my hand, blew on the food, took it in her fingers, and placed it in my mouth. Her fingers were on my lips and I started to lick them off. This was followed by a kiss laced in honey. Needless to say, things heated up and dinner had to be reheated. And I'm glad to report we've been 'cooking' ever since." *Billy's words on pine nut pie and that crucial third date with Josie, together 4 months, Kansas City, MO*

YIELDS 6 TO 8 SERVINGS

¼ cup sugar

¾ cup packed dark brown sugar

2 extra-large eggs, beaten

1½ teaspoons pure vanilla extract

1 tablespoon all-purpose flour

1 tablespoon heavy cream

8 tablespoons unsalted butter, melted

¾ cup pine nuts

1 (9-inch) pie crust

Combine the sugar, brown sugar, eggs, vanilla, flour, cream, and butter in a bowl; whisk until well blended. Fold in the pine nuts. Pour into the pie crust. Bake at 350 degrees for 50 minutes.

arabian couscous with pine nuts and raisins

works beautifully next to roasted meats

According to Jeff, "This dish benefits significantly when prepared by a cook dressed only in an apron, tied loosely around the waist."

Y I E L D S   2   T O   3   S E R V I N G S

Heat the butter in a saucepan. Add the onion and carrot; sauté until onions are translucent, about 5 minutes. Add stock and raisins; raise heat to high and bring liquid to a boil. Add couscous, stir briefly, cover, and remove from heat. Let stand 5 minutes. Stir in pine nuts and lemon juice. Season with salt and pepper.

1   tablespoon unsalted butter
½   small onion, minced
½   medium carrot, diced
½   cup couscous
1   cup chicken stock
¼   cup dark raisins, plumped
2   tablespoons pine nuts, toasted
    juice of ½ lemon
    salt and pepper to taste

springtime salad of pine nuts and avocados

light and good

While Rob and Suzie claim that "if we had any more 'aphrodisiac powers' in our life, we'd have trouble keeping our jobs," they nonetheless report that this springtime salad of pine nuts and avocados offers a "veritable symphony of textures — every taste bud on the tongue was aroused."

Y I E L D S   2   T O   3   S E R V I N G S

Tear lettuce into bite-size pieces and place in a large serving bowl. Add the avocado, tomato, pine nuts, sprouts, red onion, cheese, and cilantro. Whisk the vinegar, mustard, honey, and garlic in a small bowl. Add the oil gradually, stirring constantly. Season with salt and pepper. Add dressing to taste, and serve the remaining on the side.

½   head Butterhead lettuce
1   small avocado, peeled and chopped
1   small tomato, chopped
2   tablespoons toasted pine nuts
2   tablespoons alfalfa sprouts
¼   cup minced red onion
2   tablespoons grated mozzarella cheese
1   tablespoon minced cilantro
1   tablespoon white wine vinegar
2   teaspoons Dijon mustard
1   teaspoon honey
1   clove garlic, crushed
3   tablespoons olive oil
    salt and pepper to taste

It's true! • Take Don and Falina . . . Typical casual long-term dating situation — no commitment, no time frames, nothing. Bowling league. Movies. Party attendance. Enter pine nuts, served innocently one evening in some unassuming pesto. Bam! All the sudden they're married, have two and

anecdotal research says pine nuts

a half children, and arrange a jumbo mortgage they never plan to pay. And they're not even American! Pine nuts, of course. • Now, you're thinking, "That's pretty sketchy to conclude cause-and-effect. How can you be sure it was pine nuts?" Trust me on this. The doctor says so, reluctantly. The psychoanalyst confers. Falina's mother swears on her rosary and complains that Don and Falina could have taken a larger jumbo mortgage if they had listened to her in the first place. Pine nuts, apparently, run in the family. • More evidence? Fine. Look at Heidi and Paul. Classic invitro cataclysm. Over and over and over until Paul said one more magazine and specimen container and he was giving up, period. Heidi was in tears, walking around so very carefully after visiting the doctor, who by the way, has never failed so utterly. So they start reading fringe literature to get out of the house because . . . well, you know. Molasses.

Wheat germ. Moon phases. Vigorous exercise. Complete bed rest. The Dali Lama. The Hotel Nikko in Chicago, from which they steal a copy of *The Teaching of Buddha* that prepares them for their visit with the Dali Lama. Anti-gravity positions. Anti-gravity positions in simulated weightlessness environments.

confide. (People these days just don't appreciate neighbors, you know.) The result: Twins, non-identical. • Dave and Georgette. Helen and François. Jeremy and Jo Ann. Vern and Kelly. Debbie and Tracy. Miles and Michelle. Jennifer and John. Marie and Bobby. • But hey. I'm not going to beat my head against the

enhance nesting instinct and fertility.

Career changes. Scheduled intercourse. Varicose vein readings for fertility. Name it. Imagine it. • You guessed it. Pine nuts. And it only took one can over the course of a week, servings at breakfast and before, well, bed. Falina's mother shook her head in disbelief that Heidi's mother didn't call her sooner to

wall over this pine nut thing. Just try them. Toss them into salad or pasta whole, chop them up into dust and put them in your protein drink at the gym, roast them, toast them, juice them, crush them against your soft palatte until your tongue hurts. • I guarantee pine nuts will work for you, too. • So does Falina's mother.

Pine nuts according to Barry McCann, Pompano Beach, FL

mediterranean rice salad

½ cup basmati rice

¾ cup chicken broth

1¼ tablespoons olive oil

¼ cup chopped
   kalamata olives

2 teaspoons fresh lemon juice

1 ounce fresh arugula,
   chopped

1 green onion, minced

¼ cup pine nuts, toasted

⅛ cup feta cheese

⅛ cup grated Romano cheese
   salt and pepper to taste

"When all else fails, I buy Drew some kalamata olives. He can eat them by the gallon-full it seems. I, on the other hand, can tolerate them. We found this mediterranean rice salad a happy compromise — he got his olives and I got . . . well, let's just say the evening wasn't exactly the pits."

Carrie and Drew, dating 2 years, Portland, OR

YIELDS 2 TO 3 SERVINGS

Cook the rice in the chicken broth in a covered saucepan until tender. Fluff with a fork and spoon into a large bowl. Stir in the olive oil.

Add the olives, lemon juice, arugula, green onion, pine nuts, and cheese. Season with salt and pepper. Serve at room temperature.

angel hair pasta with fresh fennel pesto

¾ cup boiling water

1½ cups sun-dried tomatoes

½ small bulb of fennel,
   thinly sliced

1 clove garlic

¼ cup pine nuts

¼ cup fresh basil leaves

1 tablespoon fresh
   oregano leaves or
   ½ teaspoon dried

½ tablespoon lemon juice

½ teaspoon sea salt
   or to taste

1½ tablespoons olive oil

8 ounces angel hair pasta
   roasted pine nuts, sliced
   ripe olives, grated
   Parmesan cheese, black
   pepper, and oregano or
   basil sprigs for garnish

While the pesto rests and the flavors mingle, take some time to do the same with your lover. Be sure to save some energy for "dessert" — this sensuous feast may bring a glow you haven't felt before . . .

YIELDS 3 SERVINGS

Pour boiling water over tomatoes; allow to sit until soft and pliable, about 5 to 8 minutes. Drain, reserving liquid. Combine one-fourth of the fennel with the tomatoes, garlic, basil, oregano, lemon juice, salt, and olive oil in a food processor or blender. Process until smooth, adding reserved tomato-soaking water a bit at a time until desired consistency

is reached. Allow to rest while preparing pasta; if possible, let flavors blend 30 to 60 minutes. Cook pasta until al dente; drain. Combine with pesto in a large mixing bowl, tossing to mix evenly. To serve, mound pasta in the center of 2 or 3 plates, scatter with the remaining fennel, and garnish to your heart's content.

veal medallions
with pine nuts and herbs

serve with fresh bread to soak up any extra sauce

"I'd been seeing Derek for quite some time, and the relationship had reached a comfortable if unexciting stage. I decided to go for an all-out aphrodisiac meal, with the highlight being the supremely elegant entrée of veal medallions with pine nuts and herbs. I didn't tell him it was an aphrodisiac meal — I was just curious to see if they actually worked or if it were more psychological than anything. We ate until we were stuffed, moved over to the couch with our wine, and in usual fashion, turned on the tube and fell asleep. Alas, the meal had not worked. Or so I thought. Around 1:00 a.m., T.V. still blaring and dishes still dirty, I was awakened by soft, fluttery kisses. The kind I used to get every morning, but hadn't felt in probably 3 months. I guess there is something to it after all, but Derek's getting a bit suspicious about my increased interest in cooking." *Janet reflects on the power of veal medallions over Derek, together 6 years, Raleigh, NC*

YIELDS 2 SERVINGS

Season the veal chops with salt and pepper. Brown in ½ tablespoon olive oil in a skillet. Simmer for 10 minutes. Remove from the skillet and keep warm in a low oven. Sauté the tomatoes, pine nuts, capers, shallots, garlic, and herbs in the remaining olive oil for 10 minutes. Add the wine and lemon juice. Simmer for 4 minutes. Whisk in the butter. Pour the sauce over the veal. Garnish with additional pine nuts if desired.

2 (11-ounce) veal rib chops, boned and trimmed
salt and pepper to taste
1 tablespoon olive oil, divided
2 tomatoes, peeled, seeded, and chopped
¼ cup pine nuts, toasted
1 tablespoon capers
1 shallot, minced
1 clove garlic, crushed
½ tablespoon chopped fresh basil
1 teaspoon chopped fresh oregano
2 tablespoons dry white wine
½ tablespoon fresh lemon juice
1 tablespoon butter

a v o c a d o

Once again, the Doctrine of Signatures is working in full force here. The modest avocado, with its bumpy, often lizard-like skin, peels away to reveal a creamy, natural butter. Cut in half, the pear-shaped symmetry of the avocado mimics the soft, buttery curves of a woman. A striking green that earned its own name in a box of crayons, the meat of the avocado gives under the pressure of a finger and melts on the tongue in a taste all its own. • In the Aztec culture, avocados were called ahuacatl (testicle) and deemed so powerful that, as Cynthia Watson states it, "(they) forbade village maidens to set one virginal toe outside the house while the fruit was being gathered." Today, avocados run the gamut of dishes and cuisines, and more importantly, virgins now have easy access to this forbidden fruit. • The Avocado. It's not just for guacamole anymore.

sun-dried tomato and avocado fettuccine

where cuba meets italy

1 tablespoon olive oil

¼ cup diced sun-dried tomatoes

2 tablespoons sherry wine vinegar

juice of 1 lime

¼ cup chopped basil

1 tablespoon chopped green onions

2 tablespoons diced green bell pepper

1 tablespoon chopped walnuts

2 tablespoons minced cilantro

1 small avocado, diced

¾ pound fettuccine

salt and pepper to taste

½ pound bacon, cooked and crumbled

Chris and Pat share an apartment together in Austin, TX. Under certain conditions, though, their relationship has been known to cross over that understood roommate barrier into a more, shall we say, romantic arena. Such was the case with their dinner of sun-dried tomato and avocado fettuccine. According to Chris, "I fixed up a pot of this pasta and, as usual, asked Pat to join me. We usually eat in my room — the window unit's better in there, and my T.V. has a remote. We sat Indian-style on the bed, clicked on Lois and Clarke, and ate our pasta. He spent the night in my room. What can I say?"

YIELDS 2 TO 3 SERVINGS

Combine the olive oil, sun-dried tomatoes, vinegar, lime juice, basil, green onions, green pepper, walnuts, cilantro, and half the avocado in a large bowl. Toss well. Cook the fettuccine in a saucepan in boiling water for 3 minutes; drain. Toss with the avocado mixture while still hot. Place mixture on a serving platter. Top with the bacon and remaining avocado.

avocado chutney

zippy precursor to dinner

1 large ripe avocado

1 cup whole kernel corn

1 small onion, finely chopped

1 red bell pepper, finely chopped

¼ cup olive oil

2 tablespoons red wine vinegar

4 cloves garlic, minced

juice of 1 lime

2 teaspoons ground cumin

1 teaspoon chile powder

2 tablespoons chopped oregano

1 tablespoon chopped cilantro

salt and pepper to taste

I prepared this salsa as an appetizer for a modest fiesta at one couple's home. After thirty minutes of cerveza and salsa, but before we moved on to dinner, Debbie gave us the requisite grand tour of their home. As we walked into their bedroom, Debbie motioned to the bed and, knowing of the aphrodisiacs on the menu, commented, "the workbench should be getting some use tonight." The true outcome of this story will always remain a mystery to all but Debbie, Jason, and their trusty workbench.

YIELDS 4 SERVINGS

Peel and pit the avocado, then mash the avocado in a large bowl. Add the corn, onion, red bell pepper, olive oil, vinegar, garlic, lime juice, and seasonings. Mix well. Cover and chill.

"It seems to me that the anticipation of an aphrodisiac meal is oftentimes aphrodisiac enough. My significant other and I couldn't stop smiling and casting knowing glances at each other the whole time we were preparing the meal."

Karen and Rick, happily dating 6 months, NYC

hot black bean
and avocado torta

one extremely reliable sandwich

Every Monday, Wednesday, and Friday. Like clockwork, I would meet Kimber and Amy at Bar

El Jardin, our favorite open-air cafe in the *zocalo* of Oaxaca. We all three ordered the same

thing. Every single time. And we never tired of it. *Jambon torta y una lemonada, por favor.*

We would sit at our table under our umbrella and eat and drink and laugh and flirt with boys

who passed by. This is how we found our dates for salsa dancing, and we wouldn't have traded

our method for anything in the world.

YIELDS 2 SERVINGS

1 (12-inch) baguette,
   cut in half
½ pound thickly sliced ham
1 tomato, sliced
½ cup mashed black beans
1 tablespoon mayonnaise
½ avocado, thinly sliced
⅓ pound Oaxacan
   string cheese, sliced
   juice of 1 lime
1 tablespoon chopped
   cilantro (optional)

Slice each baguette in half lengthwise, then warm in a 350 degree oven until toasty. Sauté the ham and tomato slices in a skillet until slightly browned; heat the black beans in the microwave or a small saucepan until warmed through. Spread one half of the bread with the black bean purée. On the other half, assemble each sandwich with a bit of mayonnaise, slices of ham and tomatoes, avocado, cheese, a squirt of lime, and chopped cilantro. Top with the black-bean half, go outside, and enjoy your hot black bean and avocado torta. Wash it down with a fresh lemonade of mineral water, lemon juice, sugar, and lots and lots of ice.

grilled red snapper with avocado sauce

horseradish gives this sauce a kick

This recipe can be prepared with other types of fish, but for my sake, please use red snapper.

Red snapper takes me back to a beach in Puerto Escondido, an untouristy, beautiful stretch of sand,

rocks, and waves on the Pacific side of southern Mexico. Sun-burned and tired, we stumbled onto

this open-air restaurant on the quieter end of the beach. Each of us ordered the snapper — it was

prepared simply, just a whole fish grilled with lemon and cilantro. We were living a postcard

that night with the palm trees and hammocks swaying around us, and the salty air brushing

against our lips. All to say, you may borrow this memory as garnish for your grilled red

snapper with avocado sauce.

YIELDS 2 SERVINGS

Combine the fillets and wine in a shallow dish. Marinate for at least 1 hour; drain. Brush 1 tablespoon butter on both sides of the fillets. Sprinkle with the paprika. Grill 4 to 5 minutes or until done. Sauté the onion in the remaining butter in a medium skillet until tender. Whisk in the flour and salt. Add the water slowly.

Cook for 1 minute, stirring constantly. Remove the skillet from the heat. Stir in the sour cream, horseradish, and avocado. Return skillet to low heat and warm until heated through. Spoon the sauce over the fillets and sprinkle with lemon juice and parsley.

2 red snapper fillets
1/2 cup white wine
2 tablespoons melted butter, divided
1 teaspoon paprika
2 tablespoons finely chopped onion
1 tablespoon flour
1/4 teaspoon seasoned salt
1/2 cup water
1/4 cup sour cream
1 tablespoon horseradish
1 small ripe avocado, peeled and diced
1 lemon, quartered
1 tablespoon minced fresh parsley

l i b a t i o n s

"Behold how Bacchus, the aider and abettor of Venus, doth offer himself . . . let us therefore drink up this wine, that we may do utterly away with the cowardice of shame and get us the courage of pleasure." • Apuleius, *The Golden Ass* as quoted in *Secrets of Venus* • Alcohol has served throughout history as the basis for most love potions, masking foul tastes of bizarre ingredients. Today, fortunately, we typically rely on alcohol not for its hocus-pocus concoctions of wormwood and such, but for its innate aphrodisiacal powers alone. After a mere drink or two, it lowers inhibitions and allows people to do what they only fantasized as a possibility just one hour before. Whether sipping margaritas on the beach, savoring a glass of Merlot with some Camembert, or shooting body shots in a game of quarters, alcohol pushes aside the doubts, fears, and mores that typically restrain people from amorous pursuits. • Oh glorious alcohol. It transforms the could've beens into reality. Well, at least for one night.

champagne terrine

blissfully light

This recipe, graciously shared by Chef José Gutierrez of The Peabody Hotel in Memphis, will make your lover very happy. Unendingly talented, José sees to it that each dish he creates be a memorable one. Champagne terrines not excluded.

6 grapefruits, peeled
    and sectioned
7 oranges, peeled
    and sectioned
1 pint raspberries
1½ cups orange juice
8 gelatin leaves, soaked
    for 1½ hours in cold water
1½ cups champagne
½ cup sugar
⅛ cup Grand Marnier

YIELDS 4 SERVINGS

In a terrine, layer the grapefruit sections, orange sections, and raspberries, repeating the process until you reach the top. In a small saucepan, warm the orange juice. Add the gelatin leaves and cook until completely melted. Stir in the champagne, sugar, and Grand Marnier. Pour the orange juice mixture over the terrine, then refrigerate for 4 hours before serving.

jamaican fruit salsa

come . . . to the islands

According to Jen of the Jen/Henry combo, "One of the few things I remember hearing from the Ghandi of 90's love, John Gray of the Venus/Mars combo, is that the best foreplay is in the mind. It should start with a sexy intimation in the morning and fester all day until you get the chance to act out your incubating fantasies with your partner." Says Jen, "Be sure to prepare this salsa at least 2 days before the date. The flavors need the time to infuse, and just seeing it in the fridge every time I opened it was enough foreplay for any woman."

⅓ cup dark rum
3 tablespoons
    coconut-flavored rum
⅓ cup rumrunner mix
½ (10-ounce) package
    frozen strawberries,
    thawed and drained
½ cup pineapple juice
1 cup fresh strawberries
    (½ pint), divided
2 bananas, divided
1 cup diced pineapple
1 cup blueberries (½ pint)
1 cup blackberries (½ pint)

YIELDS 6 TO 8 SERVINGS

Combine the rums, rumrunner mix, thawed strawberries, and pineapple juice in a bowl. Mix ½ cup strawberries and 1 banana in the blender. Add to the rum mixture. Cut the remaining strawberries in half and chop the remaining banana. Add to the rum mixture along with the pineapple, blueberries, and blackberries; mix well. Refrigerate, covered, for up to 1 week. Serve over shortcake or pound cake. Garnish with whipped cream if desired.

wine-soaked cherries and pears over pound cake

warm and sensuous

Though not specifically covered in this book, cherries and pears have an abundance of aphrodisiacal qualities just their own, a fact all too apparent in wine-soaked cherries and pears over pound cake. The warm, succulent fruit saturated with wine will elicit a heartfelt "Oh!," the sweet, melting cream will conjure up images of The Promised Land, and all will be yours tonight and forevermore.

YIELDS 2 SERVINGS

Combine the wine, sugar, and lemon rind in a medium saucepan. Stir until the sugar dissolves. Stir in the cherries. Bring to a boil, reduce heat, and simmer for 10 minutes. Stir in the pears, and simmer for an additional 5 minutes.

Spread the pound cake with butter and toast to a golden brown. Generously spoon with fruit and juices over the cake. Serve warm, topped with a dollop of whipped cream.

1/2 cup red wine
(the better the wine,
the better the dish)
1/2 cup sugar
zest of 1/2 lemon
3/4 pound cherries, pitted
2 pears, peeled and sliced
2 thick slices pound cake
softened butter to taste
whipped cream for topping

lemon-honey spritzer

refreshing

"David and I decided to test this recipe on a Thursday night. While he mixed everything together, I pulled some chairs out into the front lawn, moved the stereo to the screen door, put in some Harry Connick, and invited our dogs Rip and Rem out to join us. We just sat, relaxing and sipping, while the street lights changed their shades of colors and the dogs chased the occasional firefly and the crickets chirped around us." *Terry reminiscing on a summer night with David and lemon-honey spritzers, together 4 years, Shreveport, LA*

YIELDS 2 TO 3 SERVINGS

Combine the lemonade and Grand Marnier in a pitcher. Add the honey, stirring until dissolved.

Stir in the champagne. Pour into glasses; garnish with strawberries.

1/2 (6-ounce) can
frozen lemonade
concentrate, thawed
2 tablespoons Grand Marnier
2 tablespoons honey, warmed
1/2 (750-milliliter) bottle
chilled champagne
fresh strawberries

"Your stature is like that of the palm, and your breasts like clusters of fruit. I said, 'I will climb the palm tree; I will take hold of its fruit.' May your breasts be like the clusters of the vine, the fragrance of your breath like apples, and your mouth like the best wine." "May the wine go straight to my lover, flowing gently over lips and teeth.

I belong to my lover, and his desire is for me" Song of Songs 7:7-10

spiked chocolate
mint espresso

chocolate mint ice cream grows up

Thomas and Patty, officially together for 3 weeks in Houston, TX, tested this recipe because
Thomas had a new espresso machine he wanted to try out. After tearing him away from the frother
(an exciting mechanism for any new espresso machine owner), Patty was able to turn his concentration
toward this creamy drink by uttering just one simple phrase: "Hon, aphrodisiacs, remember?"
Try it — it'll probably work — even for a man with a new toy.

YIELDS 2 SERVINGS

Combine all ingredients in a blender
until thoroughly combined and frothy.

Pour into frosty glasses and garnish
with chocolate shavings and mint.

2 tablespoons chopped
dark chocolate

¼ cup vodka

1 cup cold espresso

¼ cup white crème de menthe

2 tablespoons heavy cream

½ cup crushed ice
chocolate shavings and
mint sprigs for garnish

champagne laced
with raspberry

sweet bubblies

Champagne. Baci. Imported cheese. Raspberries. Saturday afternoon, in bed. According to Aaron,
"It was, without a doubt, the most sensual experience I've ever had. She fed me. She watched me.
She kissed me. She drank me with her eyes, savoring me like she did each bubble of the Möet White
star, each morsel of the chocolatey-hazelnut Baci, each wedge of the creamy cheese, each
delicate raspberry she held between her lips. I felt her effect on every inch of my body, and
I wanted to taste her, sip her, just as I had the chilled champagne with raspberry."

YIELDS 2 SERVINGS

Pour half the framboise and half the kirsch into
2 chilled champagne glasses. Tilt glasses to

coat. Add champagne and top with
1 or 2 raspberries.

1 teaspoon framboise

1 teaspoon kirsch

8 ounces chilled
extra-dry champagne
fresh raspberries for garnish

117

f i g s

If you've never had a fig before, it will not — cannot — taste, smell, look, or feel as you imagined it would — because a ripe fig tastes sweeter than any dried nugget of trail-mix fig, and a plump one smells gentler than any hyper-syruped canned version. A small, pear-shaped delicacy, its skin ranges from a soft white to a purpley-black, its flesh from a yellowish-pink to a vibrant pinkish-red. • And its feel, oh its feel. A knife slices through the fruit like soft butter. The tiny, edible seeds seem unending, weaving layer upon layer of texture and flavor within the succulent fig. All ridges work inward to a core, painting a relief portrait of the soft world of the inner thighs. When you eat a fig, you are tasting history, Cleopatra, Dionysian orgies, the Roman Saturnalia. And when its juice runs over your tongue, you are drinking pure, unadulterated sensuality.

sausage with fig sauce

spicy flavors tempered with natural sweetness

"The first meal we ever ate together was a late-night pizza. Not incredible, not exciting, not even on plates . . . maybe a little romantic. The first aphrodisiac meal we ever ate together was italian sausage with fig sauce on a bed of rice and on plates. Neither of us had ever eaten figs other than a Newton, and we weren't exactly sure of what to expect. And to be truthful, we were probably more than a little intimidated. But like obedient soldiers of love . . . we marched on. We became a little concerned when we realized that the sauce had to stay overnight in the fridge. Matthew thought, what would the sauce's parents think (The Pragmatic) — I thought, what had we committed ourselves to (The Romantic)? The actual swelling of the sauce-soaked figs brought only one thing to mind. Italian sausages with fig sauce teetered between sweet and spicy. Something familiar and not so familiar, all at once. Each bite just a little different than the bite before. And like the introduction to a promising night, full of welcomed surprise. Just the idea of the meal created an incredible, uncontrollable excitement that carried over from the kitchen to the dining room into the bedroom. We're planning on many more aphrodisiac meals for the future." *Matthew and Kelly, together 2 years, Chicago, IL*

YIELDS 2 TO 3 SERVINGS

½ cup sugar

½ cup red wine vinegar

½ stick cinnamon

2 cloves

1 teaspoon nutmeg

½ slice lemon

1 pound fresh or canned figs, drained

¾ pound bulk Italian or lean breakfast sausage

2 tablespoons white wine

2 teaspoons olive oil
salt and pepper to taste

For the fig sauce, combine the sugar, vinegar, cinnamon, cloves, nutmeg, and lemon in a saucepan. Bring to a boil. Reduce heat and simmer for 5 minutes. Add the figs. Cook for 20 minutes for fresh figs, 5 minutes for canned.

Cool in syrup overnight. The next day, cook the sausages in the wine and oil in a skillet until cooked through and wine has evaporated. Season with salt and pepper. Serve sausages on rice and top with warmed fig sauce.

creamy stuffed figs

crème de dieu

"I have to admit that I didn't believe in the powers of aphrodisiacs, especially when we begin to fight

in the middle of testing the recipes. Things can get pretty tense in his kitchen — he tends to be very

critical when it comes to that sacred part of his house. I prepared the dessert and appetizer first

while he chopped and sautéed his way through the entrée. Tensions arose when he began to

complain about the way I cut this, and the pan I put that in, etc. . . . I guess I'd just had enough,

because after one too many 'No, you're supposed to fold it in, not whisk it in' I just dunked my hand

in the cream cheese and smeared it across his face. A very bold move, I might add — it could've

gone either way at that point. Fortunately, it went to playful fighting. Then playful licking. Then

playful . . . okay, I'm drawing the line on my experience here. Suffice it to say, everything tasted

good." *Becky on her "friend" Norm, Jacksonville, FL*

YIELDS 2 SERVINGS

Combine the almonds, bacon, cream cheese, chives, and black pepper in a bowl. Make 2 slices in each fig so they open into 4 quarters. Stuff with the cream cheese mixture. Eat.

½ cup toasted almonds

4 ounces pancetta or lean bacon, cooked and chopped

½ cup cream cheese

1 tablespoon chopped chives

black pepper to taste

4 fresh figs, stems removed

FOOD COMES FIRST, THEN MORALS.

Bertolt Brecht 1898-1956 Dreigroschenoper (Threepenny Opera, 1928) act 2, scene 3

fig chutney

"In our early years of marriage, we lived for 10 years in a little white house with 2 ceiling fans and no air conditioner. But in our front yard alone, we had all kinds of fruit trees. Being parents of three children and living on a limited budget of $10,000 per year, we made use of every edible piece of fruit our trees produced. We ate it fresh, canned, candied, baked, fried. And later in the year, when we'd long since used up all the fresh and were running low on the children's favorite — canned preserves — Bud and I would turn to our dried fruit to make a version of this dip. After putting the kids to bed, we moved on to the screened porch where our 12-year-old parrot stayed (and talked incessantly), and reflected on the day's events over fig chutney and homemade ginger-ale."

Bud and Rowena, married 44 years, Vicksburg, MS

YIELDS 12 SERVINGS

Combine the figs, apricots, peaches, raisins, onion, vinegar, and enough water to cover in a small saucepan. Bring to a boil, reduce heat, and simmer for 15 to 20 minutes or until the thickness of honey, stirring frequently. Purée the pistachios, almonds, ginger, chile pepper, salt, and pepper in a food processor. (Or for authenticity's sake, use a mortar and pestle.) Add with the lemon juice to the fruit mixture, stirring well. Place in a container. Refrigerate, covered, for up to 3 weeks. Goes well any variety of ways, but particularly so with pork or lamb shish kebabs over basmati rice.

$1/4$ pound (about $1/2$ cup) dried figs, chopped

$1/4$ pound (about $1/2$ cup) dried apricots, chopped

$1/4$ pound (about $1/2$ cup) dried peaches, chopped

$1/4$ pound (about $1/2$ cup) raisins

1 small onion, finely diced

$1/2$ cup cider vinegar

$1/8$ cup toasted pistachios

$1/8$ cup toasted almonds

1 tablespoon minced ginger

1 teaspoon minced green chile pepper

salt and pepper to taste

$1/4$ cup lemon juice (about 1 lemon)

honey-drenched figs

warm juicy drippy sticky

Ineffably decadent. Use only with experienced lovers.

Y I E L D S   2   S E R V I N G S

8 figs
¼ cup honey
2 tablespoons finely
chopped pecans

Grill the figs over a low heat until heated through, turning occasionally. Warm the honey. Place the figs on individual serving plates, drizzle with enough honey to lightly coat figs, and top with pecans.

fruits in white wine

succulently mingled textures

"Laura and I have been together for more than half of our lives. It takes us by surprise sometimes. She's always had a wonderful hand in her kitchen, but sometimes I like to surprise her with a treat. This dish was a perfect combination of two of her favorites — white wine and lush fruits — and perfect for me because it is so simple." *Jim on a perfect dessert and his perfect Laura, married 32 years, Charleston, SC*

Y I E L D S   4   S E R V I N G S

¼ cup white wine
1 tablespoon sugar
4 figs, quartered
2 apricots, peeled
and quartered
2 plums, chopped
2 nectarines, peeled
and chopped
2 tablespoons coarsely
chopped walnuts

Mix the wine and sugar, stirring until the sugar dissolves. Add the fruit and toss. Refrigerate, covered, for 1 hour or longer to let flavors meld. Sprinkle with the walnuts before serving.

chocolate fig bundles

one bundle alone will not satisfy

Cheryl enjoyed making these chocolate fig bundles. "My first experience with phyllo, but not intimidating at all — I loved spreading the butter over those sheets." Frank enjoyed eating them. "This is like the sweet nectar of the gods — chocolate, almonds, figs, butter, phyllo pastry — bring it on."

Slit the figs down the side. Place in a bowl with 1 tablespoon brandy; let stand for 30 minutes. Grind the sliced almonds and grate the chilled chocolate. Combine with 1 tablespoon sugar and remaining $1/2$ tablespoon brandy in a small bowl until paste-like consistency. Stuff 1 teaspoon of mixture into each fig along with 1 whole almond. Work with one phyllo sheet at a time, keeping the others moist with a damp kitchen towel. Lightly brush the sheet with melted butter. Fold the right third over the middle then the left third over the middle (you will have a 3-layer sheet). Lightly butter the surface and sprinkle with

2 teaspoons confectioner's sugar. Cut the strip in half into 2 rectangles. Place a stuffed fig, slit side up, in the center of each rectangle. Gather the edges over the fig, pressing them together to form a bundle. Brush with melted butter. Repeat process with the other ingredients. Place bundles on a baking sheet. Bake at 375 degrees for 13 minutes or until crisp and golden brown. Remove from the baking sheet and cool. Place 2 bundles on a dessert plate. Sprinkle with confectioner's sugar and top with a dollop of whipped cream.

6   dried figs

$1 1/2$ tablespoons brandy, divided

2   tablespoons sliced almonds, toasted

$1/2$ ounce semisweet chocolate, chilled

1   tablespoon sugar

6   whole almonds, toasted

3   sheets phyllo pastry, thawed

2   tablespoons unsalted butter, melted

3   tablespoons confectioners' sugar, divided

1   cup whipped cream for garnish

confectioners' sugar for garnish

massage oils

yummy yummy juicy warm

To 1 ounce jojoba, add

21 drops (about 1 dropper full) sandlewood

6 drops ylang-ylang

5 drops steam-distilled lime

the cerebral oil of good feeling

To 1 ounce jojoba, add

13 drops francensence

6 drops patchouli

5 drops steam-distilled lime

relieve anxiety, restore balance

To 1 ounce jojoba, add

6 drops geranium

6 drops clary sage

6 drops ylang-ylang

sultry-sweet, aphrodisiac oil

To 1 ounce jojoba, add

3 drops jasmine

34 drops sandlewood

Mixing your own massage oil is a simple process to follow: simply mix 6 to 8 parts of essential oil for every 1/8 cup (25 ml or 1 fl oz) of base oil. Essential oils are available at many health food and natural food stores. (See Resources Guide on page 139 for two reputable suppliers.) Vegetable oils work nicely as the base – try almond, avocado, olive, sunflower, hazelnut, or jojoba. Mix with your signature concoction of essential oils. Store in an airtight container in a cool, dark place. • Brian Skinness with The Aromatherapy Catalogue shared some of his favorite creations above. Use these recipes straight as a massage oil or combine with bath water for a sensuously cleansing experience. As with everything else, these recipes work best when altered to your tastes, preferences, fantasies, and creativity.

a guide to

an InterCourse

aphrodisiacs know no hour

for any hour

of the day

6:00 a.m.

sunrise: *wine-soaked cherries and pears over pound cake* (page 115) You can make the cherry sauce the day before. Then when you awake, simply toast some pound cake and microwave the fruit sauce. Spread the toast with a touch of butter and top with cherries and pears and some freshly-whipped cream.

chocolate-stuffed crescent rolls (page 10) If you didn't have a chance to prepare the fruit sauce ahead of time for **wine-soaked cherries and pears over pound cake**, these croissants are a quick and delicious alternative.

9:30 a.m.

lazy saturday morning: *french toast baked in honey-pecan sauce* (page 63) This prepare-ahead recipe tastes unmercifully good. After soaking in a rich mixture of cream, eggs, vanilla, and brown sugar, the bread bakes up a puffed wonder coated with honey, pecans and yet more brown sugar..

sweet frittata with flowers (page 94) Definite breakfast-in-bed material. For that extra flourish, garnish bed sheets with edible flower petals.

noon

artichoke muffaletta (page 70) Why eat baloney when you can have this?

3:30 p.m.

afternoon delight: *bruschetta with purée of artichokes* (page 67) Feed your other half some hot, crusty bread smeared with a Mediterranean purée of artichokes, capers, parsley, and olive oil.

honey-almond delight (page 61) Bake these together with your partner — the dough tastes almost as good as the finished product.

7:00 p.m.

two rented movies and a relaxing night at home: *black bean chili* (page 77) Brown the meat, then put this chili on to simmer during the first movie. Come second showing, you can curl up with a steamy bowl of chili, some Saltines, a cold beer, and the person of your choice.

10:28 p.m.

quick — before the monologue starts: *honey-drenched figs* (page 124) It does not get any easier than this.

midnight

after the cigarette: *chocolate hazelnut truffles* (page 11) For a signature ending.

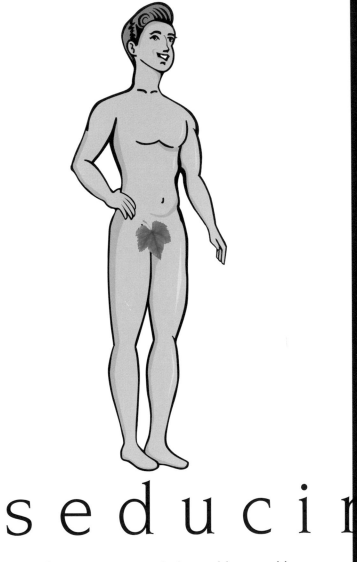

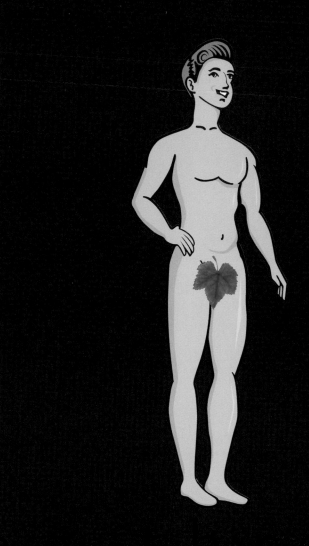

s e d u c i r

Spring: These recipes are light and breezy like the mild-weathered days of springtime.

petals in white chocolate (page 97)

basil frittata heros (page 41)

champagne grape ring (page 47)

springtime salad of pine nuts and avocados (page 101)

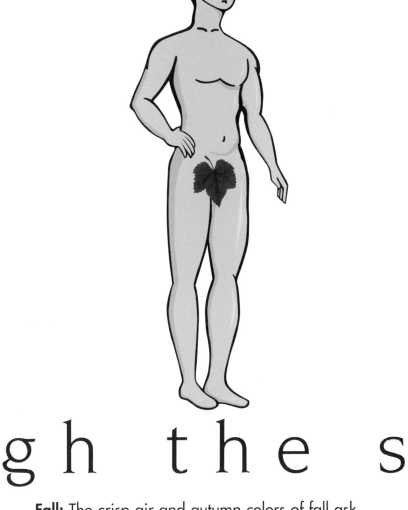

g h   t h e   s e a s o

Fall: The crisp air and autumn colors of fall ask
for cuisine that is hearty, rustic, and substantial.
Each of the following recipes complies:

herbed risotto (page 88)

honey-nut pie (page 60)

basil-eggplant soup (page 37)

sausage with fig sauce (page 120)

flirtation

whetting their appetite: the flirtation

Desire/U2...If/Janet Jackson...Pillow Talk...Roxanne...The Pick-Up Artist

grape sorbet (page 44): no bad breath after eating this and, if you garnish it with whole grapes, you can make a sensual production out of eating them

anticipation

checking out the menu: the first date seduction

I Want You to Want Me/Cheap Trick...Moonstruck

honey-peppered salmon (page 27): makes it look like you can cook, even if you can't

stages of the

copulation

an entrée to remember: it finally happens

Possession/Sarah McLachlan...Hold On I'm Comin'/Sam & Dave...Bull Durham

wine-soaked cherries and pears over pound cake (page 115): ungodly good and may actually be incorporated into the event

duration

an all-you-can-eat buffet: the, ahem, bunny stage

Black and Blue/Van Halen...Hurts So Good/John Cougar...9½ Weeks

hibiscus cooler (page 97): to refresh your parched selves (or just ditch the recipes and dip some ripe strawberries into a jar of Nutella)

exploration

heating up the leftovers: needing something new

Changes/David Bowie...Sex, Lies, and Videotape...White Palace...Henry and June...The Hunger

pasta with grapes (page 45): strange-sounding combination, but the warm grapes burst in the mouth and mingle pleasantly with the goat cheese

reconciliation

eating crow: after an argument

I Want You Back/Jackson 5...50 Ways to Leave Your Lover/Paul Simon

black russian cake (page 13): if anything will make your partner stay and/or forgive you, it's this

relationship

institutionalization

together forever

Black Coffee in Bed/Squeeze...Four Weddings and a Funeral

easy strawberry empanadas (page 50): anyone who can stay together this long deserves breakfasts like this

maturation

like a fine wine: together forever . . . and ever

When I'm 64/The Beatles...Young at Heart/Frank Sinatra...When Harry Met Sally

rosemary-scented lamb over pasta (page 87): for the mature palate

standing alone on the erogenous zones

recipes that work as well on the
body as they do on the plate

ears

lips

nipples

armpits

buttocks

genitalia

feet

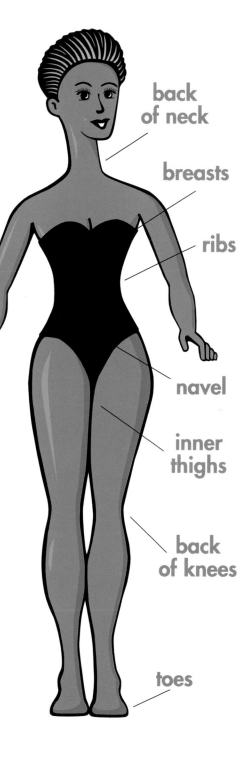

back of neck

breasts

ribs

navel

inner thighs

back of knees

toes

oysters on the half shell (page 81)

petals in white chocolate (page 97)

champagne laced with raspberry (page 117)

chocolate hazelnut truffles (page 11)

espresso cream (page 32)

honey-drenched figs (page 124)

hibiscus cooler (page 97)

creamy stuffed figs (page 121)

fruits in white wine (page 124)

jamaican fruit salsa (page 114)

filling from easy strawberry empanadas (page 50)

fig sauce from sausage with fig sauce (page 120)

sauce from wine-soaked cherries and
pears over pound cake (page 115)

champagne grape ring (page 47)

cabernet sauvignon ice (page 44)

lemon-honey spritzer (page 115)

grapes rolled in almonds and ginger (page 47)

topping from black russian cake (page 13)

strawberry butter sauce (page 51)

grape sorbet (page 44)

resources

recommended reading

For more fun reading on the subject of aphrodisiacs, turn to *Secrets of Venus*: A Lover's Guide to Charms, Potions, and Aphrodisiacs. Dr. Lee has written a most readable book — it's the kind that you pick up to read a few pages, then put down after you've read every word. *Secrets of Venus*, Vera Lee, Ph.D. $14.95, Mt. Ivy Press, P.O. Box 142 Boston, MA 02258, 617.244.2216

aromatherapy candles

For candles that can really set the stage for a sensual evening, I recommend aromatherapy candles. Unlike traditional scented candles that are made with synthetic, man-made perfumes, aromatherapy candles use only 100% pure, completely natural essential oils from plants, flowers, trees, roots, and various other botanicals. Synthetic scents mask other smells, while essential oils intermingle and physiologically alter the make-up of a smell. Because of this chemistry, aromatherapy candles can burn during a meal without interfering negatively with taste. • Aromatherapy of Rome produces, in my opinion, the best aromatherapy candles around. The candles range in size from votive up to 3 feet tall, and they carry 10 signature scents. Patchouli, my personal favorite, ages like a port wine, with its scent and patina growing stronger and richer with the passing of time. *The Aromatherapy of Rome, 18802 72nd Ave, South, Kent, WA 98032, 425.251.3555*

edible flowers

Edible flowers, though available in many supermarkets, may still be difficult to find in some places. When in need, ask your local produce manager to place a special order for you or ask for the number of the nearest edible flower supplier.

edible massage oils

As an alternative to dousing your partner with Honey Brunch Mimosas, you might want to consider the Hawaiian Love Liquors from Making Scents, a sensual fragrance company based in Maui, Hawaii. The liquors are a sensuous, natural, and edible lubricant that heat up the skin with friction or, oddly enough, a breath of air. *Making Scents, Inc., 406 Molokai Hema Street, Kahului, Maui, HI 96732, 800.861.1958*

essential oils

To scent oils, lotions, or even foods, you will need some essential oils. It is crucial, though, that these be 100% pure and natural essential oils, particularly if you are using them in cooking. Aroma Vera, a company out of California, offers an extremely reputable line of more than 90 essential oils. When working with essential oils, please treat them with respect — each one is the very potent essence of a botanic species and should be used only in measured drops. *Aroma Vera: The Power of Essential Oils, 5901 Rodeo Road, Los Angeles, CA 90016-4312, 310.280.0407*

The Bey's Garden: Aroma Vera retail boutique 310.278.8931 phone for Beverly Hills store 310.399.5420 phone for Santa Monica store

The Aromatherapy Catalogue also comes highly recommended as a supplier of carrier and essential oils. Call 800.898.PURE to request a copy.

index

works consulted

Ackerman, Diane. *A Natural History of Love.* New York: Random House, 1995.

Addison, Josephine and Diana Winkfield. *Love Potions: A Book of Charms and Omens.* Topsfield, MA: Salem House Publishers, 1987.

Augarde, Tony, ed. *The Oxford Dictionary of Modern Quotations.* New York: Oxford University Press, 1991.

Bartlett, John and Emily Morison Beck, ed. *Familiar Quotations: A collection of passages, phrases and proverbs traced to their sources in ancient and modern literature.* Boston: Little, Brown, and Company, 1980.

Brody, Jane E. "Personal Health: A New Look at an Old Quest for Sexual Stimulants." *New York Times* 4 August 1993: C12.

Cook, Adrienne. "Plant herbs; see your love life grow." *Commercial Appeal* 18 February 1996: F5.

Crenshaw, Theresa L., M.D. *The Alchemy of Love and Lust: Discovering Our Sex Hormones and How They Determine Who We Love, When We Love, and How Often.* New York: G.P. Putnam's Son's, 1996.

Fischer, Lynn. *The Better Sex Diet: The Medically-Based Low Fat Eating Plan For Increased Sexual Vitality — In Just 6 Weeks.* Washington, DC: Living Planet Press, 1996.

Fox, Marisa. "Sex Chemicals: Why pumpkin pie and lavender cause penile engorgement and chocolate is forbidden in convents." *Bazaar* February 1996: 92-94.

Heller, Linda. "Your Health: Alcohol is an Aphrodisiac." *Redbook* October 94: 33.

Herbst, Sharon Tyler. *The New Food Lover's Companion: Comprehensive Definitions of Over 4000 Food, Wine, and Culinary Terms.* New York: Barron's Educational Series, Inc., 1995.

"Housecalls." *Health Magazine* May/June 1995: 128.

Lee, Vera. *Secrets of Venus: A Lover's Guide to Charms, Potions, and Aphrodisiacs.* Boston, MA: Mt. Ivy Press, Inc., 1996.

MacClancy, Jeremy. "Food for Love." *Forbes FYI* March 14, 1994: 133+.

Watson, Cynthia Mervis Watson. *Love Potions: A Guide to Aphrodisiacs and Sexual Pleasures.* New York: G.P. Putnam's Sons, 1993.

Wegner, Fritz, and Emma Curzon. *Heaven on Earth: An Astrological Entertainment with Slides, Wheels, and Changing Pictures.* Boston: Little, Brown, and Company, 1992.

http://www.santesson.com

http://www.sugarplums.com

http://www.westwind.be/gastronomy

BEN FINK, head cheerleader • To all the models—JOSH BEARDEN, CHRISTINE CLARKE, MOLLIE CURLIN, BRYAN GREENE, DAWN

GROSSER, KORBET HAYES, KEVIN JONES, PAUL RIDDICK, AND SHEILA THOMAS — who rose well above the call of duty. Our

sincerest appreciation for your exceptionally hard work. • All contributing testers — I'll not list names to

protect the innocent (or guilty) — but we hope the food (and subsequent happenings) were as good for you as your

contribution to *InterCourses* has been for us • JEFF LEHR, who helped us move asparagus to a new dimension, among

many, many other things • CAROL BOKER, editor, proofer, tester, and best of all, friend • LEIGH ANNE MCINTOSH,

who helped bring life to this book and whose Dilbert cartoons have kept me sane • WALTER ROSE, who first uttered

the word *InterCourses* • MARY MARGARET RAGLAND and PATRICK POLLEI, who have allowed more than they should

credits

• ANGELA ANGEL, one makeup artist extraordinaire • AMY HITT, for her evil, er, eagle eye • UNCLE BILL, MARY K, AND

AUNT JANE, whose opinion I hold so highly that they might not believe it • SAJ AND JIMMY, who make the studio

a most fun place to be • CINDY FRASIER, BRAD MEADOWS, PHIL ROBERTS, AND BOB SMITH, whose generosity allowed

us to stay within budget for once • PAT AND RON, who always told me I could do anything I set my mind to

• IRENE AND SUZANNE, whose work and very self have earned our everlasting respect and appreciation • SCOTT AND

BRIAN, who gave us Pepsi, let us sit in the cold room, and became the grommeting kings of all the land

• ROGI AND CARLENE, thank you barely scratches the surface • PATTY CARROLL, GREG GODEK, JOSE GUTIERREZ, AND

BILL MITCHELL, for believing in us • PAIGE, ANDREW et al. at Mandarin Offset, who brokered their way into our hearts

INTER COURSES

an aphrodisiac cookbook

available through your local bookstore or gift shop
or by calling 800.372.2311
www.intercourses.com

For anyone who experiences some InterCourses of their own, please let us know. We welcome any such stories, as well as feedback, suggestions, corrections, questions, or favorite aphrodisiac recipes you have to offer.

Write to Martha Hopkins or Randall Lockridge
c/o Terrace Publishing, 2309 Colcord
Waco, TX 76707, 254.753.2843